The Wellness Syndrome

For Esther and Rita

The Wellness Syndrome

Carl Cederström and
André Spicer

polity

First published in 2015 by Polity Press

Polity Press
65 Bridge Street
Cambridge CB2 1UR, UK

Polity Press
350 Main Street
Malden, MA 02148, USA

ISBN-13: 978-0-7456-5560-4
ISBN-13: 978-0-7456-5561-1(pb)

A catalogue record for this book is available from the British Library.

Library of Congress Cataloging-in-Publication Data

Cederström, Carl, 1980-
    The wellness syndrome / Carl Cederström, André Spicer.
        pages cm
    Includes bibliographical references and index.
    ISBN 978-0-7456-5560-4 (hardback : alk. paper) – ISBN 978-0-7456-5561-1
(pbk. : alk. paper) 1. Conduct of life. 2. Well-being. I. Title.
    BJ1595.C623 2015
    128–dc23
                              2014022503

Typeset in 11/14 Sabon
by Toppan Best-set Premedia Limited
Printed and bound in the United Kingdom by T.J. International Ltd, Padstow, Cornwall

The publisher has used its best endeavours to ensure that the URLs for external websites referred to in this book are correct and active at the time of going to press. However, the publisher has no responsibility for the websites and can make no guarantee that a site will remain live or that the content is or will remain appropriate.

Every effort has been made to trace all copyright holders, but if any have been inadvertently overlooked the publisher will be pleased to include any necessary credits in any subsequent reprint or edition.

For further information on Polity, visit our website: politybooks.com

Contents

Introduction

Being a good person these days does not mean curbing the sinful longings of the body, mortifying the weak flesh, following your conscience and preparing through constant prayer for your departure from this life here below; it means living well. Bad cess to anyone who lets a day pass without some enjoyment!

Hervé Juvin, *The Coming of the Body*, 2010[1]

Signing the Wellness Contract

As students at the École Normale Supérieure, Sartre and his close friends had more important things to contemplate than their personal wellness. A generous observer might have described their diet as varied: a massive intake of stodgy books alternated with laxatives, consisting of cigarettes, coffee and hard liquor. In a world defined by absurdity, there were more acute issues to deal with than perfecting one's physical wellbeing. For Sartre's set, being students was to engage promiscuously with thinking, and to take risks with one's mind – not to waste time thinking about how to eat correctly.

Slightly less than a century later we find a new trend at North American universities. To shape their lives in an image of wellbeing, thousands of students across the United States are encouraged to sign 'wellness contracts'. You agree to a lifestyle aimed at enhancing body, mind and soul. If you sign the 'Campus Wellness Contract' at the University of Massachusetts, Amherst, you promise to 'maintain an alcohol- and drug-free lifestyle'. You will then get a taste of what such contracts call a 'holistic approach to living'. But then you have to give something back. You have to contribute 'positively to the community', respect 'different motivations for choosing this living option', participate in community events, and not possess drink or other drugs. And of course you need to abide by 'the philosophy of the Wellness community'.

These wellness contracts are not incidental. They are now offered by at least a dozen universities across the United States.[2] While most promote a 'substance-free lifestyle', each university has its own shtick. North Dakota takes a broad approach, offering physical, social, emotional, environmental, spiritual and intellectual wellness. At Syracuse, you get 'group trips to local parks and lakes'. You also get 'nutrition demonstrations and presentations; meditation, yoga and other forms of stress reduction; parfait nights and more'. In the more committed wellness communities, students are requested to carefully monitor their progress against the wellness goals they set out at the beginning of the year.

This may be a good thing for eager young students, at least if you ask their concerned parents. Wellness contracts make sure that students avoid harmful hedonism while encouraging other social activities (such as the mandatory 'parfait nights'). What is wrong with turning universities into year-round health spas to help students grow their bodies and minds?

The problem, of course, is that this project produces a very particular version of the student: the sanitized and straight-thinking student, who would not mix well with Sartre and his radical friends. What is likely to disappear here is a particular kind of college education where students experiment with transformative politics, take mind-expanding substances, encounter the ravages of an unhealthy diet, and experience intense and soul-destroying relationships.

It is not just some North American college students who have promised to pursue wellness. Today, wellness has become a moral demand – about which we are constantly and tirelessly reminded. To be a good person, as Hervé Juvin reminds us in the epigraph, is to constantly find new sources of pleasure. It means turning life into an exercise in wellness optimization. At work, we are kindly offered a place on 'wellbeing programmes'. As consumers, we are required to curate a lifestyle aimed at maximizing our wellbeing. When we engage in boring activities, such as washing up at home, we should think of them as improving our mindfulness. Even baking a loaf of bread is now recast as a way of nurturing our wellbeing.

In other words, wellness has wormed itself into every aspect of our lives. A few decades back, wellness was the preserve of small groups of alternative lifestylers. Today, wellness has gone mainstream. It dictates the way we work and live, how we study, and how we have sex. We find it even in the most unexpected places, such as the Ashland Federal Correctional Institution, Kentucky, where prisoners undergo wellness programmes and learn about nutrition, exercise and how to deal with stress.[3]

Our concern in this book is not with wellness *per se*. Our concern is how wellness has become an ideology. As such, it offers a package of ideas and beliefs which people may find seductive and desirable, although, for the most part, these ideas appear as natural or even inevitable. The ideological element of wellness is particularly visible when considering the prevailing attitudes towards those who fail to look after their bodies. These people are demonized as lazy, feeble or weak willed. They are seen as obscene deviants, unlawfully and unabashedly enjoying what every sensible person should resist. 'The fat, the flaccid, and the forlorn are unhealthy,' Jonathan M. Metzl writes in *Against Health*, 'not because of illness or disease, but because they refuse to wear, fetishize, or aspire to the glossy trappings of the health of others.'[4] When health becomes an ideology, the failure to conform becomes a stigma. Smokers are regarded as not just threats to their own personal wellbeing, but a threat to society. As we will see later in this book, some workplaces have moved from banning smoking to banning smokers, shifting the focus from an unhealthy activity to an unhealthy individual.

This ideological shift is part of a larger transformation in contemporary culture where individual responsibility and self-expression are morphed with the mindset of a free-market economist. To stop smoking is not so much about cutting down on your immediate expenses, or even extending your life expectancy, as it is a necessary strategy to improve your personal market value. The 'obese body', Lauren Berlant writes, 'serves as a billboard advert for impending sickness and death'.[5]

People who don't carefully cultivate their personal wellness are seen as a direct threat to contemporary society, a society in which illness, as David Harvey puts it, 'is defined as the inability to work'.[6] Healthy bodies are productive bodies. They are good for business. And the same goes with happiness. Assuming that happy workers are more productive, corporations devise new ways to boost their employees' happiness, from coaching sessions and team-building exercises to the recruitment of Chief Happiness Officers. The result, as Will Davies has put it, is that now 'wellbeing provides the policy paradigm by which mind and body can be assessed as economic resources'.[7]

The Wellness Syndrome

The focus of this book is on wellness as a moral imperative. Although this argument has been made by a number of theorists, no one has put it so elegantly as Alenka Zupančič. In *The Odd One In*, she calls this biomorality. This is what she writes:

> Negativity, lack, dissatisfaction, unhappiness, are perceived more and more as moral faults – worse, as a corruption at the level of our very being or bare life. There is a spectacular rise of what we might call a bio-morality (as well as morality of feelings and emotions), which promotes the following fundamental axiom: a person who feels good (and is happy) is a good person; a person who feels bad is a bad person.[8]

Biomorality is the moral demand to be happy and healthy. It is a familiar remark, which brings to mind the central ideas of the self-help movement. The same term appears in Slavoj Žižek's *In Defense of Lost Causes*. Even though he leaves this intriguing term unexplained, it is clear that the moralizing turn of wellness is an extension of what he elsewhere calls the 'superego-injunction to enjoy'. What we encounter here is not the punitive paternal superego which tells us 'no, don't do that'. Rather, the superego tells us to have fun, to express our true selves and to seize every opportunity in life for enjoyment. But as we will see in the course of this book, this command is not designed to improve our wellness, or to unleash enjoyment. It is often unclear what this demand actually implies, whether we are demanded to cautiously pursue moderate pleasures or to violently plunge into excessive enjoyment. We will deal with that issue later, but for now it is enough to say that turning enjoyment into an obligation is not entirely good news. '[T]he very injunction to enjoy', Žižek writes, 'sabotages enjoyment, so that, paradoxically, the more one obeys the superego command, the more one feels guilty.'[9]

Wellness has undergone a similar transformation. Today wellness is not just something we choose. It is a moral obligation. We must consider it at every turn of our lives. While we often see it spelled out in advertisements and life-style magazines, this command is also transmitted more insidiously, so that we don't know whether it is imparted from the outside or spontaneously arises within ourselves. This is what we call the wellness command.

In addition to identifying the emergence of this wellness command, we want to show how this injunction now works against us. And this is what we call the wellness syndrome.

The Oxford English Dictionary gives us two definitions of the word 'syndrome'. The first refers to 'a group of symptoms which consistently occur together'. Keeping this definition in mind, we can say that the wellness syndrome refers to symptoms such as anxiety, self-blame and guilt – to name a few. As we shall see throughout the book, the wellness syndrome is based on an assumption about the individual, as someone who is autonomous, potent, strong-willed and relentlessly striving to improve herself. This insistence that the individual is able to choose her own fate, we argue, provokes a sense of guilt and anxiety. We are thought to be in control of our own lives, even in situations where circumstances are not in our favour. Jobseekers experience this in difficult economic times when they are told not to mention the crisis, but instead to focus their attention on themselves. Finding a job, they are told, is about will-power and choice.

Choice is usually seen as a positive thing. However, it 'brings an overwhelming sense of responsibility into play', Renata Salecl writes in her book *Choice*, 'and this is bound up with a fear of failure, a feeling of guilt and an anxiety that regret will follow if we have made the wrong choice'.[10] When wellness goes from being a general idea of feeling good to something that we ought to do in order to live truthfully and righteously, it takes on a new meaning. It becomes an impossible demand that reconfigures the way we live our lives. Obsessively tracking our wellness, while continuously finding new avenues of self-enhancement, leaves little room to live.

When the body has become the ultimate object of your life, a new Archimedean point, the surrounding world is seen as either a threat or a balm. Our body determines where we live, whom we spend time with, how we exercise, and where we go on holiday. Part of this corporeal obsession is our deep fascination with what we put in our mouth. Indeed, eating has become a paranoid activity, which is not just intended to bring momentary pleasures through taste. It puts your identity to the test. Eating correctly is thought to be a way to cook up a happy and prosperous life, free from stress and despair. To eat correctly is an achievement, which demonstrates your superior life-skills. As the cultural significance of this activity has grown, the market for expert advice has boomed. In a style that blurs new-age sophistries with scientific discoveries, dietitians and celebrity chefs have been elevated to priestly status. When we cannot find meaning in our lives, a rare culinary experience becomes a stand-in. One *New York Times* restaurant critic recently released a book describing how meals prepared by eight women chefs 'saved her life'.[11]

Such obsessive attention lavished on diets and cookery reminds us that eating has taken on a new meaning. As Pascal Bruckner puts it, 'The dining table is no longer the altar of succulent delights, a place for sharing a meal and conversation.' Instead it has become, 'a pharmacy counter where we keep an eye on our fats and calories and conscientiously eat food reduced to a form of medication'.[12] All of the pleasures that we used to indulge in are now pleasures with one ultimate objective – to improve our wellness. Wine or fat are perfectly fine, if you can fit them into your wellness plan. As Steven Poole suggests in *You Aren't What You Eat*, food has become our present-day ideology.[13] For foodists, eating is more than just a lifestyle; it is a metaphysical adventure. Having lost our faith in politicians and priests, Poole argues, we now turn to celebrity chefs and nutritionists to find answers to the big questions. And unsurprisingly, given the importance that foodism attributes to eating correctly, the obsession with this – orthorexia – has become a new idiosyncratic disorder.

Opening the dictionary again, we see that a syndrome can also mean 'a characteristic combination of opinions, emotions, or behaviour'. The wellness syndrome characteristically combines an obsession with the body with a burning desire for authenticity. This may seem counterintuitive: being preoccupied with your body is normally seen as superficial. However, improving one's body is too often seen to be a way of improving one's self. In *Better Than Well*, Carl Elliott describes how technologies 'from Prozac to face-lifts are routinely described as tools of self-discovery and self-fulfillment'.[14] Rather than being narcissistic, the search for personal health and authenticity is regarded as a moral responsibility. 'Many people today feel *called* to pursue self-fulfillment,' Elliott writes, 'to devote themselves single-mindedly to a career, for example, or to cultivate their looks through severe diets and punishing workouts at the gym, even if it means ignoring their children.'[15]

When we are trapped by the wellness syndrome, we become what Simon Critchley calls passive nihilists. 'Rather than acting in the world and trying to transform it,' he explains, 'the passive nihilist simply focuses on himself and his particular pleasures and projects for perfecting himself, whether through discovering the inner child, manipulating pyramids, writing pessimistic-sounding literary essays, taking up yoga, bird-watching or botany.'[16] Where does our preoccupation with our own wellness leave the rest of the population, who have an acute shortage of organic smoothies, diet apps and yoga instructors? Withdrawing into yourself and treating the signals of your body as a good-enough ersatz for universal truth has become an increasingly appealing alternative to thinking soberly about the world.

1

The Perfect Human

Having no hope of improving their lives in any of the ways that matter, people have convinced themselves that what matters is psychic self-improvement: getting in touch with their feelings, eating health food, taking lessons in ballet or belly-dancing, immersing themselves in the wisdom of the East, jogging, learning how to 'relate', overcoming the 'fear of pleasure'.

Christopher Lasch, *The Culture of Narcissism*, 1979[1]

The Life and Death of Coaching

For the Brooklyn police, 3 June 2013, was just another day. Neighbours had complained about the foul smells coming from a nearby apartment. At the scene the police found two decomposing corpses, belonging to a couple of middle-aged adults – one male, one female. They had committed suicide by placing Helium-filled plastic bags over their heads – devices known in euthanasia circles as 'exit bags'.

This seemed to be another double-suicide story, bound to pass silently. But the occupation of the two dead – Lynne Rosen, 46, and John Littig, 48 – was going to add an unexpected twist. Their deaths made international headlines when it was revealed that they were both radio show present-ers and, more intriguingly, life coaches. Their particular area of expertise: happiness. The unanswerable question that now began to circulate was: why would a happiness-preaching life-coach duo commit suicide?

The radio show was called *The Pursuit of Happiness* and ran on WBAI-FM. The listeners were encouraged to embrace the possibilities of change. In one widely circulated out-take from their radio show, the hosts reflect on the former first lady Eleanor Roosevelt's advice to 'do one thing every day that scares you', the point being that 'stepping outside of your comfort zone is very important', because we must 'start to get comfortable with change'. Rosen also recorded an inspirational rap video, where she encouraged viewers to become 'the person you always wanted to be'. The couple ran their own life-coaching business, Why Not Now, where clients were offered help to 'foster and encourage your inner strengths, identify hidden and untapped resources, and put you confidently on the path to designing the life you've always wanted to live'.[2]

The themes of Why Not Now are familiar to anyone with a passing acquaintance with self-help, and its vaguely for-mulated commands: be happy, nurture your body, cultivate a positive attitude, connect to your deepest inner emotions. And coaches, like Rosen and Littig, are important adherents of this movement.

Although relatively unknown a few decades ago, life coaching has now become a common occupation. There are about 45,000 coaches world-wide, and the industry as a whole generates $2 billion a year.[3] The background of coaches varies wildly, from people with little or no education to people with Ph.D.s in clinical psychology and many years of work experience. It is also common for highly experienced members of other professions, such as psychoanalysts, to rebrand themselves as coaches, expecting their business to become more lucrative as a result.

One of the appeals of coaching is that anyone can do it. There are some reputable institutions, such as Harvard University, which offer certificates in coaching. But the training is generally very fragmented with an array of private providers offering short online courses.

You can now find coaches to help you perform better at work, get a new job, deal with difficult personal matters, buy a house, improve your health, or strengthen your relationship with God. You can even consult so-called 'wantologists', who are professionally trained to help you figure out what you actually want.[4]

The International Coach Federation, a key industry body, describes coaching as 'partnering with clients in a thought-provoking and creative process that inspires them to maximize their personal and professional potential'. A good coach needs to 'honor the client as the expert in his or her life and work and believe every client is creative, resourceful and whole'.

What makes coaching so appealing is that it knows no boundaries, and that it can come in playful, experimental forms. An example of this would be the increasingly popular technique known as equine assisted coaching, which drafts in horses to help clients unlock their hidden strengths. Wisdom Horse Coaching, based in Minneapolis, offers this service, helping managers to develop their skills by learning how to lead a horse.[5] Another unconventional example of coaching is the weekend programme 'Escape from the Man Cage' run by Martha Beck, where groups of disillusioned men are taken through a range of exercises from animal tracking to fire-building. In one exercise the men are told to 'think of themselves as animals and to use only their sense of hearing to try to locate and tag each other — all in an effort to awaken the senses and instincts presumably deadened by desk jobs and smartphones'.[6]

Despite the apparent lack of focus, all forms of coaching rely on a specific idea, inherited from positive thinking, which maintains that the individual has the ability to unlock her own inner potential. In his diagnosis of 1970s North America, Christopher Lasch connects this idea to the human potential movement and its relentless focus on self-awareness and human growth. This theme is not hard to find among today's life coaches. As one coach puts it, 'You and I are already whole, resourceful, capable and creative.'[7] 'Coaching', we learn from another practitioner, 'is about finding your inner expert to reach your goals.'[8] Unlike the more esoteric brand of new-age therapists, life coaches sell their services as practical and result-oriented. Preserving the original idea of unlocking the inner self, they have added more athletic motifs such as peak performance. To become yourself, you have to become better – and to become better, you have to reach your goals. Self-exploration and self-discovery is morphed into self-actualization and self-enhancement.

Feelings of malaise led one of Martha Beck's clients to join a five-day coaching trip to Africa (costing $10,000). Following this journey, the client discovered that the problem was not her job as a paediatric surgeon, but her attitude. She realized that 'I was no longer hating what I was doing. All of the so-called problems that I thought I had in terms of not fitting or being good at it or good enough – I realized they were in my own head and not outside of me.'[9] This advice, given by Beck, echoes the messages of Rosen and Littig, the two Brooklyn life coaches we met at the beginning of this chapter. In their radio show, they encouraged their listeners not to look outside of themselves, but to turn their gaze inwards.

There is something very attractive about the idea that we all have a hidden potential within. There is also something alluring about self-enhancement: that we can become better versions of ourselves, emotionally and spiritually. But there are good reasons to remain sceptical. In her critical analysis, the sociologist Arlie Russell Hochschild notes that coaching implies a strange form of 'outsourcing'. She argues that we now outsource those intimate aspects of our lives that we previously performed ourselves. We hire a coach to help manicure our online profiles in the hope that this will land us a date. We turn to coaches to ask what we actually want in life. When we begin to consult coaches in this manner, we render our everyday reality into an extended realm of expertise. As our intimate life is outsourced to professionals, Hochschild argues, we lose something fundamental. It seems as if we get ourselves into a circular quest for perfection, where, to afford paying for more advice, we need to work longer hours. This is the irony, or what we may call the coaching trap: 'The more anxious, isolated and time-deprived we are, the more likely we are to turn to paid personal services. To finance these extra services, we work longer hours. This leaves less time to spend with family, friends and neighbors; we become less likely to call on them for help, and they on us.'[10]

But there is another reason to be suspicious about coaching. As well as outsourcing our intimate lives to (self-certified) experts, coaching leads to the insourcing of responsibility. One of the central motifs running through most life-coaching interventions is that you must take responsibility for your own life and your own sense of wellbeing. But the flip side is that we now have to blame ourselves for all conceivable problems, whether they are about relationship breakdowns, job losses or serious illnesses. Wellness is a choice – *my* choice – and as such also my own responsibility. The nagging awareness of this responsibility provokes an intense feeling of anxiety. The coach's job, Renata Salecl points out, is to temporarily defer this anxiety. When talking to the coach, we displace some of our insecurities. But the coach is not an authoritarian father figure who tells us what to do and how to behave. In Salecl's words, it is crucial that the coach 'does not appear to be or behave like an authority who demands to be obeyed'. Instead, he or she should be more like a 'benevolent helper whom the individual has chosen to listen to'.[11] This is where we can see the other side of the coach. The coach no longer defers the client's anxiety, but pushes the tyranny of choice back onto the client. One of the standard techniques used by many coaches is to ask their client something along the lines of: 'imagine that money or other barriers were not an issue, what would your life be like in ten years' time?' Questions like these entice the coached to play a fantasy game. But typically this becomes a cruel game when coaches try to get their coachees to 'see' that the only real barrier to achieving these fantasies is themselves.

By pushing the anxiety back onto the individual, the coach is not so much resolving the trauma of choice as intensifying it. And this is the essence of the ideology of life coaching, Salecl claims: it 'insists that existential crisis and anxiety represent just a plain lack of willpower or a crisis of confidence'.[12] In the absence of an external authority, the responsibility falls on the individual. The authoritarian father disappears, but only to reappear in a different shape: not as an angry man with flared nostrils shouting at you, but as an invisible figure integrated into your brain. What makes this figure harder to deal with is that he never leaves you alone. The angrier and more frustrated you get with him, the more violently you will turn inwards.

A similar point is made by Christopher Lasch. He claims that in the wake of the political turmoil of the 1960s (Vietnam, Watergate, etc.), many people repudiated politics and institutions they viewed as paternalistic, instead focusing on individual projects, such as, in his words above, 'taking lessons in ballet or belly-dancing' or 'immersing themselves in the wisdom of the East'. But this does not lead to a more comfortable and forgiving existence. 'On the contrary,' Lasch notes, 'it encourages the development of a harsh and punitive superego.'[13] Punitive self-hatred, then, is the flip side of self-fascination.

What Lasch is suggesting here is that rather than addressing issues of subjective anxiety, a therapeutic culture adds fuel to the narcissistic fire. Other people are interesting only insofar as they can teach you more about yourself. With 360-degree feedback you can integrate other people's opinions for the purpose of self-enhancement. This is a deeply lonely world, Lasch continues, where you are surrounded by ideals and self-images. And what's worse is that this intimate relationship that you have developed with yourself is bound to take a violent turn. As Slavoj Žižek points out in *The Ticklish Subject*, '*imaginary* ideals, such as success and bodily fitness, often turn back on the self. The illusion that we are beyond society and capable to shape ourselves in the image of perfection results in a return of a ferocious superego.'[14] This is a special kind of superego, which is not saying no, or what we can or cannot do. Like the coach, this is a figure that tells us to do more, to be better, to be ourselves. Meanwhile the superego remains disappointed, constantly pointing out that we could have performed much better. 'So we have a subject who is extremely narcissistic,' Žižek writes. '[F]ar from allowing him to float freely in his undisturbed balance, however, this narcissistic self-enclosure leaves the subject to the (not so) tender mercies of the superego injunction to enjoy.'[15]

When listening carefully to this postmodern superego that tells us to enjoy, we should recognize that the message is not sincere. Rather, it is an ironic command, because what the superego knows is that enjoyment is ultimately impossible to attain, especially if it is being expressed as a command.

And yet, this is the command that we continue to see and hear at every turn in our daily lives, whether it is in self-help books or corporate team-building exercises. Why do we continue to search for enjoyment in this desperate manner, when we know at the outset that the result will be disappointing? Perhaps we are not looking for more enjoyment. We are just seeking to blend in. We should acknowledge that the coached self, who has been taught to take full responsibility for her own life-choices, is the self that is often best equipped to meet the contradictory demands of present-day capitalism: to be simultaneously extroverted and introspective, flexible and focused, adaptable and idiosyncratic. In other words, coaching does not just seek to improve people's wellbeing, or to teach them how to enjoy more. It is a technique aimed at reshaping the self. We will now meet the person who has taken this message to heart, and fully accommodated the demands of extreme performance, flexibility and innovation. Her name is the wo/man of now.

The Wo/man of Now

At every historical moment we find an image of the perfect human; and contemporary capitalism is no exception. We meet him in a short television advert launched during the 2013 Australian Open: 'I'm a new-age man. I'm ageless but not ageist.' The words flow smoothly from this lightly bearded man with bedroom eyes as we watch him confidently striding through the Café Latte precincts of a modern city: 'I'm free-range, free-spirited, free-willed…but on a leash.' He is a self-aware, freedom-loving man with an environmental consciousness: 'I push the envelope, push the button, push a pram, push it real good.' He sports casual clothes, short hair and a man bag: 'I wear the pants, I wear aftershave, I wear the blame and I wear it well.' He is a social animal, always networking, always on the go: 'I'm tweeting, posting, hosting, sharing, linking, liking.' He is a performance-poet-management-consultant, who knows how to treasure the small things in life: 'I'm house proud, a house husband, I like a house party, now I'm in the dog house. I'm a barbecuing, meat-eating, sausage-sizzling, prawn-peeling, salad lover.' In short, he is the man of now: 'I'm international, inter-connected, inter-continental, I'm into everything.'

After giving his elevator pitch, our new-age man reaches his target – a car. He slips in and disappears. The vehicle is accidental, of course. It could have been replaced by any other product that is vital for the man of now, who is into everything. What is on sale here is a particular self: flexible, action-oriented and endlessly changing.

But this hyper-individualized network-spanning self is not the sole preserve of men. Women can be like this too. We meet the man of now's female counterpart in a twin commercial: 'I'm a woman of my time; on time; behind time.'

She is a *Sex and the City* feminist who is not ashamed of her career focus: 'I climb the corporate ladder. I've got a ladder in my stockings. I can't wait. Don't have time to wait.' She employs her erotic capital but does not say no to a succulent cake: 'I put on weight. I lose weight. I wear a skirt. I wear the pants. I wear heels, and I wear them out.' Like the man of now, she is always connected: 'I'm texting, typing, LOLing, OMGing.' But most importantly, she does not conceal anything from the world: 'I don't internalize,' she explains, 'I vocalize.'

These super-contemporary figures have not just reached their human potential. They have learnt how to *vocalize* it too. They are flexible, multifaceted and connected. They can become anything and everything, at any time. Work-life, home-life: there is no difference. They can be communist-capitalist, feminist-misogynist, queer-homophobe, caring-careerist, vegetarian-meatlovers with a bent for slow-cooked fast-food. No painful trade-offs need to be made. Everything is possible, all the time.

The wo/man of now is a product (or perhaps symptom) of what is often termed a new spirit of capitalism. We will explain what this means in a moment, but to emphasize the relative novelty of this spirit one only has to go back about half a century to find a dramatically different culture of capitalism. To illustrate this, consider John Brack's iconic painting *Collins St, 5 p.m.* from 1955. This famous image portrays life among the organizational men and women in a large Australian city. It captures a familiar moment: when worn-out office workers finally clock off for the day and head home in droves. These are glum-looking people in dirty colours all rushing in one direction – presumably from their bureaus to the railway station. Although we may find remote signs of individuality on their faces, they strike us as a mass of standardized drones all parading to the beat of a bureaucratic machine. There is no spark of subjectivity in their eyes. Instead their faces are weathered by years at the desk. Here, there is no room for fantasies of self-actualization.

Now, consider again the upbeat hipster-careerist, for whom the greatest fear is to become an indistinguishable part of an insipid mass. Together, this new generation of flexible workers constitutes not a mass of conforming selves but a mass of contending selves. Moreover, they are not split between home and work, but perpetually stuck in a fluid work–home hybrid. They are not a lonely crowd, but connected loners. Not bureaucrats, but authenticrats.

These images capture two dramatically different spirits of capitalism. *Collins St, 5 p.m.* depicts life under the Fordist spirit of capitalism – a mass of relatively affluent, efficiently organized, standardized bureaucrats. They have a place called work and a place called home; they enjoy certainty, and they share common experiences. But this life of the salaried job and the daily trudge down Collins Street at 5 p.m. comes with a loss: the loss of individuality and authenticity. The repetitive rhythm of work and life provokes a sense of disenchantment and boredom. While under Fordism life is safe and certain, it is also dull. For the wo/men of now, things are different. They often lead an eventful life where they are centre stage of their own identity drama as they shuttle between the grand uncertainties of work, life, love and pleasure.

In *The New Spirit of Capitalism*, Luc Boltanski and Eve Chiapello explore this transformation in close detail.[16] How is it that we have become so obsessed with features such as flexibility, fluidity, connection and self-expression? What makes these ideals so attractive? In their analysis, Boltanski and Chiapello go back to the Great Depression of the 1930s and the ensuing social unrest in order to identify the emergence of Fordist capitalism. At this particular time, various movements came together around a new social demand, namely security. It was also security, together with efficiency, productivity and rationality, that was at the roots of the Fordist spirit. These are the values that are pictured in Brack's *Collins St 5 p.m.*

Of course, these values were not universally shared. Critics would make the case that Fordism produced lonely and alienated people, entirely disconnected from whatever their desires may have been. It condemned people to live and die according to the same pattern: safely, efficiently, soullessly.

During the late 1960s, this indignation grew stronger. Many people began requesting something beyond mere security, such as meaning, authenticity, self-expression and genuine human connections. In short, they wanted to escape the straitjacketed Fordist experience. Boltanski and Chiapello argue that these demands would later become incorporated into a new generation of management-speak. Nowadays, the former slogans of activists abound in the workplace: creative work, flexible projects, network organizations, visionary leadership, intensive communication, liberation management, and so on. With the advent of the new spirit of capitalism, work underwent a dramatic transformation. No longer assumed to be boring, alienating or dehumanizing, work became seen as an avenue for people to explore their untapped potentials and to express themselves. The artistic critique against capitalism – that corporations make us inauthentic – is now inverted and used by firms to launch a new cultural ideal, partly based on artists and their presumed creativity, entrepreneurial ability and counter-cultural edge.

Today we find this artistic ideal in many places, most visibly in the creative industries. At the dawn of the new millennium, IT start-ups expended at least as much effort emitting an image of counter-cultural cool as they did delivering products and services. Often they would move into abandoned warehouses and fill them with designer furniture and deviant dudes cruising around on skateboards. This was long before Google. But the culture of cool is also a culture of overwork. In his account on Razorfish, a legendary firm of the first generation of cool IT start-ups, Andrew Ross notes how, by eradicating the difference between life and work, workers were kept at the office at all times. Ross labelled this 'geeksploitation'.[17]

While Razorfish disappeared with the dot.com bubble, these 'cool' workplaces have survived. In a recent list of such workplaces[18] we can read about Red Bull's London office with slides instead of stairs, and someone who has converted a vintage trailer into a home office. But more than being cool, the office of the new spirit of capitalism is distinguished by its contempt for hierarchy. One of the most talked-about companies in recent years is the Las Vegas-based shoe-selling company Zappos. In late 2013, the company announced that it would become a 'holocracy'. Doing away with traditional managerial hierarchies and job titles, it created 400 'self-managing circles'. To find the right people, with 'the right attitude', prospective employees are asked questions such as: 'on a scale of 1 to 10, how weird are you?' One HR officer described how she 'had three vodka shots with Tony [Hsieh, Zappos's CEO] during my interview'.[19] Other bizarre details about Zappos include the celebrations of the CEO's fortieth birthday party, when a group of employees hit the town and all got matching tattoos.

But what contemporary employment conditions really share with the artist is precariousness. In the new spirit of capitalism we might find workplaces that emphasize individual expression. But they are not particularly secure. In *Non-Stop Inertia*, Ivor Southwood points out that precarious employment relationships have become the 'dirty laundry of large organizations' from which 'chief executives and productivity gurus avert their nostrils'.[20] These positions last from month to month, week to week, even hour to hour.

Some are on zero-hour contracts, where they have to be ready for work at all times. They also need to accept that their work can be cancelled at any moment, without notice.

In his analysis of life in precarious work, Southwood lists the many jobs he has had, from caring and cleaning to warehousing. The only thing they have in common is that they can be cancelled without notice. When working in one warehouse, realizing he can lose his job at any time, he finds himself continually asking: 'Could this be my P45 moment?'[21] He describes how he and his co-workers 'hated the place and despised everything it had come to stand for, and yet we were terrified of being "set free" into an economic vacuum where we would struggle to find work and have to present ourselves indiscriminately to other potential employers as similarly enthusiastic, compliant and flexible'.[22] While the precarious labour relations make workers constantly feel existentially vulnerable, there is a particularly cruel twist of fate, Southwood points out: although they are in a precarious situation, they are required to hide these feelings and project a confident, upbeat, employable self.

And this is where we come back to the wo/man of now. S/he is not just the archetypal figure of the new culture of capitalism. S/he is the image that we all need to emulate in order to get by. We must be on the move, constantly. We are tweeting, posting, hosting, sharing, linking, liking. The flexible worker's wall is never dry. What is crucial is not what you have achieved, but what you can become. What counts is your potential self, not your actual self.

What we often fail to note here is that the demand to be authentic, positive and self-expressive is not just directed to the few employees at Zappos or Google. Most of those who face these demands are working elsewhere, in warehouses, in health care or mundane office jobs. Even the unemployed are exposed to these demands (as we will learn in chapter 4). The seeming incompatibility between upbeat self-coaching jargon, on the one hand, and the precariousness of work, on the other, is perfectly captured in the fly-on-the-wall documentary *The Call Centre*. Set in the South Wales city of Swansea, which is plagued by unemployment and social malaise, this documentary shows how young people are forced to fully express themselves in the workplace. Following the slogan 'happy people sell', the manager, Big Nev, assembles new employees on the first day of their job for a communal singalong. They sing frantically, as they know that Big Nev has previously fired those who don't join in.

At the heart of these precarious employment relationships lies the harsh insistence that choice is an individual matter. We are constantly told that we choose our appearance, our friends and our work. We can choose to be positive, productive and on-message. Temporary employment is often presented as a way of maximizing choice, not just for the employer, but also (somewhat strangely) for employees. According to Renata Salecl, this state of constant uncertainty encourages us to 'act like a corporation: to make a life-plan of goals, make long-term investments, be flexible, restructure our life's enterprise and take the risks necessary to increase profits'.[23] All of this requires constant choices about who we are, but also a hidden message that we may be making the wrong decisions. Salecl argues that this injunction to choose entails profound experiences of anxiety. Things could always be otherwise, if only we choose otherwise. Such awareness opens up a kind of existential whitespace, which hits us with panic. In the face of this tyranny of choice, we seem to crumble. It is there, in all situations, from the most mundane ones, such as choosing cheese, to the most profound, like choosing a career path or life partner. The utter contingency and undecidability of choice confronts us as a horror. And what is even more horrific is that we will be responsible for the decision (even if it is made for us). So if it all goes wrong, we only have ourselves to blame. Choosing between their many possible selves, the wo/men of now are also wracked with anxiety. It is no wonder that the two commercials cited above are so disjointed and disorienting – the wo/man of now is in the flow, the flow of anxiety.

Search Inside Yourself

The most popular training course offered at the Googleplex (Google's headquarters in California) is not in programming, leadership or accounting. It is a course that teaches Google engineers 'mindfulness'. Since its inauguration, the course, entitled 'Search Inside Yourself', has been attended by over 1,000 employees. The initiative came from Chade-Meng Tan, a 41-year-old ex-software engineer with the official title of 'Jolly Good Fellow'. In his book *Search Inside Yourself*, Mr Tan describes the goal of the course as helping participants 'optimize' themselves by increasing their emotional intelligence.[24] By listening carefully to their bodily signals, participants can develop what Mr Tan calls 'high-resolution perception of their emotions'. This entails developing better intuition, which can give a kind of psychic foresight.

'We need an expert,' Tan tells his audience. 'That expert is you. This class is to help you discover what you already know.'[25] After being asked to look inside themselves, participants are guided through a set of exercises most life coaches would already be familiar with. In one, participants are asked to share three of their core values. In another, they are asked to spend seven minutes writing about how they envisage their lives. In yet another, they are asked to focus on their breathing for two minutes. As Tan claims, '[S]ustainable happiness is achieved simply by bringing attention to one's breath.'[26]

The widespread popularity of the phenomenon has made mindfulness grow into an industry. One can now find mindfulness apps, mindfulness training programmes, mindfulness coaches and even an emerging science of mindfulness.

The mindfulness industry regularly organizes events, such as the 'Wisdom 2.0' conference, where well-known speakers are invited and smaller start-ups demonstrate their wares. But the enthusiasm for mindfulness has extended far beyond Californian computer programmers and new-age entrepreneurs. A more unlikely institution that has recently begun to harness the techniques of mindfulness is the US Marine Corps. With a technique called 'mind fitness training', it hopes to reduce the amount of post-traumatic stress and high suicide rates among soldiers returning from combat. At

Camp Pendelton in California, 160 Marines are 'taught to focus their attention by concentrating on their body's sensations, including breathing, in a period of silence', after which they are sent into 'a mock Afghan village with screaming actors and controlled blasts' to practise their new-found mindfulness techniques.[27]

The core techniques of mindfulness have been practised for several thousand years. Most books on mindfulness like to remind the reader of these deep historical roots. References to Buddhism and Christian mysticism are commonplace. What is unique about 'contemporary mindfulness', however, is how it is packaged. Here we find a strange hybrid of Eastern spiritualism, self-help, neuroscience, techno-fetishism and postmodern business jargon, all delivered in a corporate-casual style. In a book like *Search Inside Yourself*, we seamlessly move between ancient Tibetan wisdom and double-blind clinical trials with MRI scanners.

Herein lies the appeal of mindfulness. Apart from having a clear goal (making you more productive), and helping you get in touch with a deeper, more spiritual side of yourself, it is supported by science. As pointed out in a *Huffington Post* article, mindfulness advocates often make unsubstantiated claims.[28] Sure, there may be evidence suggesting that mindfulness can help individuals reduce stress and anxiety, but the grander claims appear less grounded. For instance, there is no strong evidence that mindfulness will increase efficiency, reduce absenteeism, improve 'soft skills' or make organizations kinder, more compassionate and more sustainable. This is not necessarily a major concern for those who sell books and courses on mindfulness. What matters is not the quality or the reliability of the evidence. What matters is that it *feels* true, and that it has the aura of science. This form of overblown promise is typical of what Ben Goldacre calls 'Bad Science'.[29]

But perhaps the most compelling element of mindfulness is its promise to act as a panacea for many of the endemic problems of post-industrial capitalism, such as anxiety, stress and existential insecurity. Ron Purser and David Loy point out that 'corporations have jumped on the mindfulness bandwagon because it conveniently shifts the burden onto the individual employee: stress is framed as a personal problem, and mindfulness is offered as just the right medicine to help employees work more efficiently and calmly within toxic environments.'[30] For them, mindfulness becomes a way of shifting the responsibility for social ordeals back onto the individual. So rather than addressing the root causes of these feelings it provides us with 'tools' for self-help. But what is perhaps the cruellest twist in the story is that stress, anxiety and feelings of depression are not seen as a creation of the external work environment. Instead they are a creation of your own lazy and unfocused mental habits. If you feel stressed by having too much work, or insecure at the prospect of an upcoming restructuring exercise, all you need to do is clear out the cacophony of negative thoughts, breathe deeply and focus.

In addition to pushing many of the structural insecurities of the modern economy back onto the individual, the doctrines of mindfulness also reinforce the idea that impermanence, constant fluidity and change are not just the effect of an economy that creates increasingly precarious employment relationships and fractured personal relationships. No, the claim is that impermanence is an immediate reflection of the basic nature of reality. In an article published in the *Journal of Management Inquiry*, we are asked to recognize that 'impermanence is the quality of experience that everything is shifting, going to pieces, slowly dissolving, rising and falling and that moment-to-moment experience is all there is.'[31] By emphasizing the fleeting nature of the world, the authors help normalize erratic corporate restructurings, which fundamentally affect the livelihoods of many thousands. This is also the point that Ivor Southwood makes: that the experience of generalized insecurity has become pitched as perfectly normal, as 'the nature of things'.

While mindfulness subscribes to a vision of reality in which everything is in a constant state of flux and fluidity, it throws us back into the only immediate reality we know – our own body. And that is often the mantra of mindfulness courses: that we need to listen to the wisdom of our body.

When we ignore our reason and other basic aids to decision-making (such as empirical evidence, the opinions of others and social norms) and instead begin 'listening to our body' to make judgements and decisions, the body becomes what Hervé Juvin has called a 'truth system'. 'In it,' he writes, 'we place all our hopes, from it we expect a reality which elsewhere is leaking away.'[32] When everything else – external reality, institutions, relationships – is regarded as a transient moment, it is only our body and its stealthy wisdom that we can rely on. By interrogating our bodies and listening to their most subtle signals, we are told we can find the truth, not just about who we are, but about what constitutes the good life. Judgement should not be made through careful rational analysis; it should come from the gut.

If the body becomes a kind of 'truth system', then it is not particularly surprising that we become so obsessed with defending our bodies against even the slightest disturbances. Anything that violates our body, even in the most spurious way, comes to be perceived as a threat of the highest order. One of the greatest examples of that violation today is smoking.

Why Everyone Loves to Hate Smokers

Smoking is not just bad for your health; it is bad for your career too. In 2011, the *New York Times* ran a feature article describing how some American hospitals have developed increasingly tough employment policies targeted at smokers.[33] Dissatisfied with the results of previous non-smoking policies, they had now changed tactics from banning smoking to banning smokers. This meant that even a cigarette outside of the premises, before or after work, would not be tolerated.

To make sure that they were hiring a totally smoke-free person, prospective employees were subject to urine tests, similar to those used to detect drug-users.

To justify such invasive and punitive measures, these employers said they were interested in the wellbeing of their employees. Of course, they were also concerned about the economic costs of smoking, such as decreased worker productivity and higher health-care costs. They claimed that previous efforts involving slightly 'softer' measures, such as offering smoking cessation programmes or banning smoking within the workplace, had not delivered the desired results. Ever since the prestigious Cleveland Clinic stopped hiring smokers in 2007, other hospitals in the United States have followed suit.

On the face of it, this debate is about economics and health. Smoking is costly (for society and for employers), and it is bad for health. However, smokers have also become a curious subject of interest, in both private and public discussions. Indeed, it is perfectly acceptable to ridicule and satirize smokers. They are often viewed as comic and disgusting, rather like Patty and Selma, the two heavy-smoking, constantly coughing aunts in *The Simpsons*. But why is this the case? Why do smokers appear to be funny? And why do they trigger so much moral indignation? We often forget that only a decade or two ago, smokers and smoking were the most normal thing in the world. You could light a cigarette without anyone paying attention. Offices, cars, aeroplanes, shops – wherever you went you would find ashtrays strategically located. And the health-care sector was by no means immune.

Recent employment policies, which recommend banning smokers rather than smoking, are part of a longer history in which smoking has been either banned or regulated. Famously, Nazi Germany was the first nation to impose smoking bans in public places. It was also under the Nazi regime that the link between smoking and cancer was first established. As Robert Proctor points out in *The Nazi War on Cancer*, 'German tobacco epidemiology was, in fact, for a time, the most advanced in the world, as were many other efforts of the anti-tobacco effort.'[34] Nazi Germany offers an interesting example of how science and moral indignation can sometimes feed into one another. Smokers in Nazi Germany were viewed as second-class citizens, almost as low in rank as alcoholics, who, we mustn't forget, were among the first to be sent off to the concentration camps in the mid-1930s. It was clear that smoking was antithetical to the ideology of racial hygiene and bodily purity, and scientific evidence pointing in that direction emboldened people to express already existing prejudices in a violent manner.

Over the course of the last seventy years, research has been able to map out the dangers of smoking in great detail. Meanwhile, we have also seen the emergence of progressively more restrictive bans. Today, in most developed economies it is prohibited to smoke in the workplace, and it has become increasingly common to ban smoking from public places such as pavements and parks. What is interesting about these bans is that they largely clash with the neoliberal spirit of individual choice. As free men and women, we should be able to do what we want with our bodies. We should have the freedom to light up a cigarette if we feel like it. To over-come this contradiction, between freedom, on the one hand, and paternalism, on the other, smoking bans have been justi-fied mainly in medical terms. Hence, it is not about restrict-ing smokers' freedom, but about safeguarding the freedom of those who may unwillingly inhale the smoke. An interest-ing aspect of the discussions leading up to the ban in restau-rants was the potential threat that smoking would pose to those working in that environment. This is interesting because the rights of restaurant-workers, such as to a minimum wage and to legal employment contracts, are often otherwise ignored.

Rather than improving the conditions for workers in the industry, a more plausible explanation why smoking became banned in restaurants is that it no longer carries the positive cultural connotations it once did. The tobacco industry was immensely successful in enhancing smoking with a magic aura. In the 1950s, a cigarette was the inevitable accessory for the elegant woman walking into a luxurious restaurant, and the freedom-loving cowboy. Today, these images are largely gone from the Western world (although the tobacco industry is engaging with ethically dubious strategies to encourage people in poorer countries to begin smoking).[35] Instead of being a sophisticated expression of freedom, smoking is now seen as a ridiculous activity worthy of condemnation. But the shift is not just about smoking; it is more directly related to smokers, who are now viewed as both morally and aesthetically regressive.

This is a point made by Chris Grey and Jo Brewis.[36] They argue that medical knowledge imperceptibly morphs into a moral language. We go from a medical statement that smoking is bad for your health, to the shorthand version that smoking is bad; followed, finally, by the assertion that smokers are bad.

There is an important political dimension to this, which is only rarely noted. Chantal Mouffe, in *On the Political*, argues that the defining feature of our contemporary post-political situation is not just the disappearance of the political. 'What is happening', she writes, 'is that nowadays the political is played out in the *moral register*.'[37] This moral register serves numerous purposes: it separates us from them, and it tells us right from wrong. Meanwhile, we can act as if we are not talking about politics at all. We are just passing legitimate (and scientifically supported) claims: that, say, smoking is stupid and that smokers must be stupid too. This is a central point to moralization: that it has a depoliticizing effect. In other words, through a moral register we can stigmatize smokers (and others), all the while telling ourselves that this is nothing to do with politics; it is simply about morality.

Such depoliticization is absolutely central to the wellness syndrome, whereby happiness and health become the fundamental criteria for what passes as a moral life. Morality, here, is not just to do with your relation to other people; it is concerned with the relation to yourself, and especially to your own body. Renata Salecl points out that an important aspect of all pervasive choice is people being forced to take responsibility for their own health care. In this kind of setting, 'the doctor no longer plays the role of an authority, advising what course of action is best for the patient; now he simply tells the patient what their options are, leaving them to make a decision and to give (or refuse) their informed consent.'[38] This is not necessarily experienced as a kind of liberation from medicalized control. Instead, 'health problems become the individual's ultimate sin. Like the employee who is made to feel guilty for losing his job because he hasn't been able to search for a new one before the current one ends, sick people feel guilt for not preventing illness.'[39] Failing to take responsibility for one's own health through not smoking becomes not just a potential spark for bodily failure, but also a moral failure.

This moral register is applied to our everyday life, ranging from what we eat to how we dress to how we have sex. All of these activities are evaluated in relation to whether they are good or bad. And as the line between the public and the private vanishes, these mundane activities have attracted more attention. It is not that politics extends into the private sphere (recall the old feminist slogan 'the personal is political'). Rather, we can see the opposite movement taking place, whereby larger public concerns become rendered as questions of individual taste and morality. The personal life of politicians is now described in great detail, assuming that it is in the bedroom, bathroom or kitchen that we might discover the true answer to their politics. This ranges from the sexual proclivities of Silvio Berlusconi to the music tastes of David Cameron. Every week brings new examples of this moral privatization of politics. Sure, this obsession with the private is not entirely new. There has always been a fascination with the lifestyle minutiae of our politicians. Even so, it is arguably only with the advent of mass media – in particular television – that the lifestyle of politicians has become a central battleground in which the struggle over the common good is fought.

Creating a better world is no longer an issue of public deliberation. It becomes a question of personal lifestyle choices. People's deep cynicism about major institutions becomes matched with a kind of naïve enthusiasm about making their lives better through enhancing their lifestyle. Direct action is the order of the day. And more often than not, the target of this direct action is one's own body. The tools in such campaigns become fitness programmes, diets, lifestyle television shows and positive thinking programmes. The great figures are no longer politicians, activists or intellectuals. They are celebrity chefs, happiness gurus and enthusiastic entrepreneurs. The great watch-words of these campaigns are health and happiness.

2

The Health Bazaar

In our culture, fat is evil. Eating it or wearing it, feeding it or bearing it is a sign of some moral deficiency. Aesthetically, physically, and morally, fat is a badge of shame.
                                  Richard Klein, *Eat Fat*, 1996[1]

The Work-Out Ethic

'Our most important currency is not time but energy. It is easy to keep people at work around the clock. Minds are willing. You have to fight the biology.'[2] This is how one senior investment banker described his workplace when interviewed by the academic and ex-banker Alexandra Michel. Like his colleagues, he would work 120 hours a week, sleep very little and have almost all of his bodily needs catered for by the company. For one junior banker, the bank is 'like an artificial world. Instead of going home, after 5:00 P.M. people here just switch into leisure clothes, turn on the music, and the firm orders dinner for you. Ironically, you end up working a lot more because it is so convenient.'[3] One banker described his work as being 'like a psych experiment where the light is always on'.[4]

After following hundreds of investment bankers over a period of nine years, Michel found a striking pattern in how employees coped with the demands of their work. In the first three years, bankers perceived their bodies as something that had to be overcome to keep up with their gruelling schedule. One respondent described how he 'did everything I could to numb my body so that it would not get in the way'.[5] Attempts to overcome the weaknesses of the flesh worked for some time. But in their fourth year of employment, the bankers' bodies began to 'fight back'. Previously mild-mannered individuals would now fly into unwarranted fits of rage. One respondent described how he 'stormed toward the taxi, but the door was locked. The driver wanted to unlock it but couldn't because I kept operating the handle. I became so furious that I kept banging against the windows like crazy, swearing at the poor guy.'[6] Another banker told Michel he suffered frequent injuries from his after-midnight jogging routine. Many described an overwhelming sense of numbness, obsessive consumption of food and pornography, and systematically shirking obligations to family and friends. In their sixth year, the bankers who still remained had stopped beating their bodies into submission. Instead they had found a new technique, which drew distinctly on a 'new age' register of being 'mindful', observing the flow of situations, and attending to and trusting their body. They were 'listening to their body' and treating it as if it were a 'trusted friend'. Those in harmony with their body could continue to endure the work conditions.

The struggle to keep energy levels up and remain productive is not limited to investment bankers. Michel notes that there are many workplaces where people must be extreme performers, often through denying or dominating their bodies. She mentions 'high-stakes finance jobs, hospital-based medicine, software engineering, consulting, law, and also elite athletics, academia, and art'.[7] But it is not just these relatively privileged workers who are coerced to neglect elementary bodily needs. Many people in routine service work, manufacturing and agriculture habitually work beyond safe limits, denying themselves something as basic as sleep.

In *24/7: Late Capitalism and the Ends of Sleep*, Jonathan Crary argues that sleep is one of the last barriers to capitalist production and consumption.[8] The zone of sleep had previously been outside of the relentless circulation of images and demands to work. However, with various innovations, ranging from industrial lighting of cities in the early nineteenth century to contemporary social media and productivity drugs like Modafinil, this space has steadily been eroded. The result is a constant state of wakefulness, not just among a few privileged investment bankers, but among the wider population.

Being 'always on' creates its own challenges. As we have seen from Michel's study, the single most important barrier is the body itself. While the mind may want to overcome natural barriers like sleep, the body fights back. This is the central challenge for the agent of 24/7 capitalism: to struggle against the corporeal enemy of productivity and to train his or her body in the way Michel's bankers did. The importance of such callisthenic interventions is underscored in an article published in *Harvard Business Review* by two fitness trainers turned management advisers, Jim Loehr and Tony Schwartz.[9] For them, busy executives are 'corporate athletes'. Real athletes, we are told, have a far easier ride than their corporate cousins. 'The average professional athlete', Loehr and Schwartz write, 'spends most of his time practicing and only a small percentage – several hours a day, at most – actually competing.' This stands in stark contrast to most executives, who spend 'almost no time training and must perform on demand ten, 12, 14 hours a day or more'. But the difficulties of executive life go beyond this: 'Athletes enjoy several months of off-season while most executives are fortunate to get three or four weeks of vacation a year. The career of the average professional athlete spans seven years; the average executive can expect to work 40 to 50 years.'[10] To continue performing, corporate athletes need to strive towards what these 'coaches' call an 'ideal performance state'. And this requires behavioural interventions, such as dietary changes (eating five or six times a day, drinking water regularly), weight-lifting twice a week, staying mentally focused and breathing deeply, developing a regular sleep regime, visualizing moments of peak performance, and taking 'time out' to reconnect with a deeper sense of purpose. By doing this, the authors assure us, corporate executives are able to 'feel strong and resilient – physically, mentally, emotionally, and spiritually – [and] perform better, with more passion, for longer'.[11]

Many companies have followed this trend and are now encouraging their employees to get into a state of peak performance. A recent survey by RAND found that just over half of US employers with more than fifty staff offer some kind of workplace wellness programme.[12] Another survey found that 70 per cent of Fortune 200 companies provide employee fitness programmes.[13] In total, US employers spend about $6 billion a year on such programmes. This growing popularity is partly to do with the fact that these initiatives are often tied up with employees' health insurance. To get access to insurance, employees are often required to participate in a wellness routine.

According to a World Economic Forum report, these kinds of wellness schemes typically include components such as diet groups, diet counselling, cafeterias with health food, exercise breaks at work, on-site gym facilities and smoking cessation.[14] The focus of these schemes is exclusively put on the body. By going to the gym and stopping smoking, employees can improve not just their health, but also their corporeal image. Fat or a non-typical body shape is, as Richard Klein points out in the epigraph above, a badge of shame. Employees can show their determination to be not just healthy, but morally and aesthetically responsible human beings, who are easy to get along with. As such, these initiatives are also assumed to create a stronger sense of corporate belonging. At Patagonia, the sportsware company, employees frequently go running together.[15] A flexitime policy lets them pursue outdoor activities in the middle of the day, which are proudly championed in a book by the CEO with the title: *Let My People Go Surfing*.

Another new management health fad is the walking meeting. In a recent TED talk, the technology executive Nilofer Merchant warned that 'sitting has become the smoking of our generation'.[16] Echoing the concerns of many others, she points out the significant amount of time we spend sitting each day (9.4 hours for the average North American) and the negative health consequences this has. To combat the sin of sitting, she suggests business people should 'kill their meeting room' and instead opt for 'walking and talking'. This has clear health benefits, creates better connections between team members, and turns people's attention away from the potential escape of their mobile devices. Walking meetings are also thought to do much more. An article in the *Huffington Post* notes that 'little diversions, like catching sight of a beautiful bird (or, let's be honest, an artfully organized garbage can, if you're a city worker), could be the spark your brain has been waiting for to unleash that brilliant idea.'[17]

A further step towards blurring working and working out is found in new pieces of office equipment: the treadmill desk and its close cousin, the bicycle desk. The treadmill desk allows employees to walk at a slow pace – often one to two miles an hour – while they continue to work at their desk. It was invented by James Levine, an endocrinologist, who had become concerned about the health risks of people's increasingly sedentary lifestyles. Attaching a treadmill to a workstation, Levine wanted to get people working out while working. Google, Microsoft and Hyatt-Marriott have purchased these work(out) machines. They have also proved popular with many freelancers working from home. One person told the BBC that by using the treadmill desk 'you're seriously multitasking.'[18] Another treadmill desk owner described how he found it difficult to push himself to go to the gym, so he would frequently walk for five hours a day while doing his work as a software developer. He lost 35 pounds, gained swollen feet and produced a blog about it in the process.

A similar invention, the bicycle desk, is pitched at the eco-conscious hipster. One such desk, created by a New York State start-up called Pedal Power, allows users to work, exercise and generate the electricity for laptops. In the words of one of Pedal Power's founders, the device has the added benefit of helping to 'connect people to the energy they use' and 'understand how precious energy is and how hard it is to come by'.[19]

On the face of it, measures ranging from workplace well-ness programmes to the treadmill desk are all relatively harmless. They seem to be a reasonable way to help people with sedentary lifestyles to remain fit, healthy and produc-tive. Some may even say that companies are doing it for our own good. But, if we look a little closer at attempts to make the workplace healthier, we notice it is not just about creat-ing a healthier, happier and more productive workforce. In fact, the benefits of wellness programmes are often dramati-cally overestimated. One study pointed out that there is a limited take-up, and that those who do participate show relatively minor health improvements.[20] Another US study suggested that while employers make some savings through employee health programmes, this is often achieved through shifting costs of health care onto those who are more likely to be sick (that is, the poor).[21]

If the strict utilitarian benefits of workplace health initia-tives are somewhat unclear, perhaps there are other reasons why so many corporations are enthusiastic about corporate work-outs. One explanation is that making employees engage in fitness routines helps firms to sculpt the workforce. Pound-ing away on a treadmill desk is more about the production of an ideal worker than achieving productivity goals. This creates a strong and compelling connection between the fit employee and the productive employee. People who smoke, are overweight or sedentary are automatically seen as inactive and unproductive. The image of the idealized worker has transformed from the workaholic Stakhanov of Soviet Russia into the exercise-addicted corporate athlete who is able to carry out a hard day of creative labour while happily leading an exercise class after work.

When work becomes exercise and exercise a form of work, we begin to notice the blurring of boundaries between what have previously been separate activities. Taking a walk while talking about budgets, cycling at your desk or even surfing during lunch all fuse moments of leisure and labour. Far from being a barrier to taking care of our health, work becomes a time and place where we can engage in self-care. But working out also becomes a kind of labour of keeping an idealized corporate body in shape.

An intriguing experiment to break down the boundary between work and non-work can be found at Scania, the Swedish truck manufacturer. In their study of the company, Mikael Holmqvist and Christian Maravelias document how the company operates a policy of the '24-hour employee'. This means 'Scania cares for its employees, both on and off the job. We try to help them live healthier. Our interest and care for the employees does not end when they leave work.'[22] The programme features many standard workplace health measures like providing employees with fitness facilities (employees received a fitness centre as a present for the one hundredth birthday of the company), and conducting 'lunch walks' (twenty minutes of Nordic walking, for which the company had received awards). But there is a much more extensive apparatus of measures designed to engineer fit and healthy workers. All this is administered by a large workplace health team (made up of psychologists, medical staff and behaviour experts) who work closely with the human resources department and industrial engineers to ensure overall industrial efficiency. One health promotion worker recognized that the company 'cannot command employees to eat properly'.[23] What they can do, however, is to create what the researchers described as 'far-reaching norms about how they should work but also how they should live and relate to themselves in order to remain healthy and productive'.[24] To this end, they had developed an advanced wellness programme, targeting the *whole* employee. It included activities such as health profiling, improvement groups, a health school and 'health talks', where employees are asked questions such as: What are your eating habits? Do you exercise? Do you smoke? How do you spend your leisure time? What are your sleeping habits? Are you lonely? What do you want to do with your life?

These measures might seem invasive. But surprisingly, many employees found it a positive opportunity to improve themselves. One of the participants in the Scania programme told the researchers: 'In these times when people are laid off due to the global financial crisis, you need to stay fit, and the health profile helps you do so.'[25] For him, staying fit was a kind of unemployment insurance; it allowed him to remain an attractive employee, not just for his present employer, but for other potential employers if he happened to be laid off.

A striking feature of this kind of self-work is that it will never be finished. As with the forward-looking employee at Scania, you need to remain fit for possible challenges in the future. Zygmunt Bauman, in *Liquid Modernity*, points out that 'the pursuit of fitness is a chase after a quarry which one cannot describe until it is reached; however, one has no means to decide that the quarry has indeed been reached, but every reason to suspect that it has not. Life organized around the pursuit of fitness promises a lot of victorious skirmishes, but never the final triumph.'[26] As such, corporate exercise programmes never stop. After the walking meeting, you return to the treadmill desk, followed by more work-out sessions in the evening. Fitness requires constant work, especially as one has to be prepared for unnamed future challenges. In this sense, fitness produces an experience of, as Bauman writes, 'perpetual self-scrutiny, self-reproach and self-deprecation, and so also of continuous anxiety'.[27]

This continuous anxiety is not limited to the shop-floor or walking meetings on the company campus. It also continues after official working hours, when the corporation is no longer watching over your shoulder. Given the deep connection between becoming an ideal employee and being fit, we might say the work ethic has been replaced by the workout ethic. Instead of committing oneself to ceaseless work and a frugal life, as was the case with someone seized by the Protestant work ethic, we now encounter corporate athletes who commit themselves to constant exercise and health monitoring. While nineteenth-century Protestant entrepreneurs used hard work as a way of staving off the horrific question of whether they were going to spend their afterlife in heaven, today's corporate athletes work out to suspend the question of whether they are the kind of active and energetic employees their company (or indeed any other) might find attractive. Instead of hard work being the price of entry to heaven, working out has become the price of today's secular heaven – continued employment.

The Guilty Pleasure of Dieting

Reverend Rick Warren is a Pastor at the Saddleback Mountain Church, a typical mega-church in Southern Orange County, California, with a congregation of 30,000 people. In 2010, while baptizing 858 people, his thoughts began to wander. When he had got up to about 500 baptisms, he was suddenly struck by a new thought: 'We're all fat.' As he described it to a *New York Times* journalist, this 'wasn't a very spiritual thought', adding that 'I know pastors aren't supposed to be thinking that when they're baptizing, but that was what I thought: we're all fat. I'm fat, and I'm a terrible model of this.'[28] This revelation led Rev. Warren to lay down a challenge to his congregation the following week: 'OK guys, I've only gained like 3 pounds a year. But I've been your pastor for 30 years. So I've got a lot of weight to lose. Does anybody want to join me?'[29]

A few months later, Warren launched an evangelical diet named the 'Daniel Plan'. This 'groundbreaking healthy life-style programme founded on biblical principles' draws its narrative from the story of Daniel, a wealthy Jew who, along with three companions, had been deported to Babylon, and interned in the King's court. To abide by Mosaic law, Daniel denied offers of the King's fine fare such as meat and wine and restricted his diet to vegetables and water. This religious narrative is coupled with many of the typical thera-peutic themes of postmodern mega-churches such as per-sonal development.

One can easily recognize the language of self-help here. Just consider the titles of the spiritual lessons offered as part of the Daniel Plan: 'For good health, confess your sins', 'Eliminate negative self talk' and 'Put down the chocolate and pick up your bible'. The support of a number of celebrity health experts (including a Columbia University cardiologist with a television show, a 'world famous' physician and a metabolism expert) has added a scientific feel. This blend of evangelical religious narrative, celebrity health expertise and a commitment to success through self-development has made the Daniel Plan deeply appealing to the large neo-evangelical market in the United States and beyond. An estimated 150,000 people are following this diet.

But fasting is by no means limited to evangelical North American Christians. It has become a popular theme among many iconic dieting fads in recent years. The central proposi-tion that they share is that you can be as permissive as you want some days, as long as you impose clear limits other days. Periods of asceticism are alternated with periods of excessive enjoyment. Perhaps the most well-known formula-tion of this principle can be found in the so-called '5:2' diet. This basic formula was articulated by the British physician and journalist Michael Mosley, who produced a BBC docu-mentary promoting the benefits of intermittent fasting. Fol-lowing the wild popularity of this documentary, he paired up with a dietary writer and published the best-selling book

The Fast Diet.[30] They claimed that having two days a week with very restricted intake of calories, followed by days when you eat what you like, results in weight loss and the improvement of many important biological functions.

Stepping back from the actual practices, we can begin to consider the ideological and anthropological dimension of diets. The first thing to note is that dieting has an intimate connection to excess. As the sociologist Bryan Turner points out, dieting only becomes possible or desirable in a society where there is an excess of calories available.[31] He traces the rise of modern rationalized dieting back to early modern England and the work of the physician and early diet guru George Cheyne. In a confessional manner, Cheyne described how he over-indulged in the pleasures of early eighteenth-century London and grew to the impressive size of 448 pounds. He then shed his girth through a diet of milk and vegetables. Although initially aimed squarely at a small class of sedentary professionals in London suffering from the results of an excessive intake of food and a lack of exercise, Cheyne's ideas soon spread. They were picked up by wider moral reform movements, first the Methodist Church and later the National Efficiency Movement, which directed nutritional advice towards those further down the social order. What these movements tried to do was to link a healthy diet and healthy body with morality. According to Turner, this had the effect of 'producing a sober and athletic population whose healthy bodies would not disrupt production as a result of illnesses following "irrational" eating and drinking habits'.[32]

Cheyne's own story follows a familiar narrative arc from an unnatural life of excesses to a blissful state of nature. Often, diets promise a return to an imagined 'pure' state before the excesses of food corrupted us. On the one hand, we have, as Turner puts it, 'the frugality of man in the innocent state of nature'. On the other, we have 'the excesses of man in civilized society'.[33] When trapped in the society of excess, 'the route out of the condition was one of asceticism and diet', which could 'restore the mind and body to health'.

This is a central theme in dieting. The Daniel Plan refers to an original state of biblical times. The 5:2 diet refers to the famine and feast cycles of our prehistoric ancestors. The Palaeolithic diet goes even further back in time by suggesting we emulate the habits of cavemen by only eating things we can kill or forage. Fruitarians champion an 'Adam and Eve' diet that recommends only eating what you would find in the Garden of Eden: fruit, vegetables, nuts, and the like.

Diets typically promise an escape from the excesses of the modern world and a return to a more authentic life. But the road the dieter must walk to make this escape is marked by modern modes of instrumental control and regulation. Most diets provide precise and highly regulated tables prescribing what and when to eat. They also give a clear trajectory of which foods are to be consumed when. Turner uncovers this strict rationalization and micro-discipline in the early modern dietary interventions of Cheyne, who drew up extensive tables for his readers. Contemporary diets require similar kinds of micro-regulation and self-surveillance, such as counting calories, carefully monitoring meals, keeping track of your body mass index, attending regular confessional meetings with other dieters, employing diet coaches, subjecting yourself to regular weigh-ins, checking in to dieting websites, reading dieting books, keeping a diet journal and recording your daily dietary intake on a computer-based application (which you should then share on social media). According to one feminist critic of diets: 'Since the innocent need of the organism for food will not be denied, the body becomes one's enemy, an alien being bent on thwarting the disciplinary project.'[34]

This experience of control is vividly captured by the former Weight Watcher Cressida Heyes, who describes how she had 'never been in another adult milieu where discipline was applied to such tiny behaviors and deviance greeted with such serious and inflexible responses from the staff'.[35] Heyes was puzzled by how rapidly her fellow Weight Watchers were drawn into the disciplinary techniques offered by the company (such as calorie counting and a public weigh-in). As she describes, they quickly lost 'all sense of proportion' and became utterly obsessed with the smallest details of weight change and dietary compliance. Submitting themselves to this tight disciplinary regime, they changed not just their behaviour, but also their self-understanding. Daily practices of self-management were not seen as an imposition. They were a source of satisfaction and personal empowerment, a way to becoming oneself. In the words of the weight-loss organization Slimming World, they helped you to 'be the person you really want to be, now and forever'.

Monitoring what you eat is not a strictly private affair. As we have already seen in this chapter, health promotion has become a widespread practice among corporations. Google famously hired a corporate chef, whose mission it was 'to keep people near one another and their desk; prevent them from developing poor eating habits that would diminish productivity; eliminate the time they would otherwise spend going out to lunch and worrying over plans; create a sense of togetherness'.[36] But perhaps his most important role, as he saw it, 'was to create the illusion you were not at work but on some type of cruise and resort'.[37]

Attempts to discipline employees' diets are by no means limited to high-tech firms. An increasingly ubiquitous feature of mundane organizations is health talks. In her work on counselling of overweight employees in Danish municipalities, Nanna Mik-Meyer found that these therapy sessions placed great emphasis on employees' own responsibility to maintain healthy habits. As one manager crudely put it: 'We want the individual to take the greatest possible responsibility for his own life and his personal situation...his fatness.'[38] By taking responsibility, it is assumed that employees can find their true selves hidden under layers of fat.[39] In one typical intervention, a health consultant exhorts an overweight participant in a weight-loss retreat to locate his willpower: 'The cookie is always beckoning you...and if you want to cope with that, you'll have to give your willpower a bit of space....where is your willpower inside you? Where? Is it in your knee? In your side or your back, where is it?' The participant responds, 'I'm damned if I know.'[40]

Another example is found at Scania, the Swedish truck manufacturer that we visited earlier in this chapter, which offers 'employees a healthy and nutritious breakfast and lunch; but also inspire[s] them to eat healthier at home'. Through the company 'health school', employees considered to be 'at risk' are trained in techniques of healthy living. The company also operates the 'Scania BMI programme', which offers a comprehensive set of interventions designed to help employees manage their lifestyles. One employee explained that 'doing sports, eating well, being outdoors, and in general, taking care of your health has almost become the norm here.'[41] But it also means, in the words of a behavioural expert working for the company, that 'if you never read anything, just sit around watching stupid things on TV, and if you only eat fast-food and never do any exercise you might end up as a rather unattractive and useless employee.'[42]

What is characteristic of these forays by companies into dietary regulation is that they want to avoid appearing like they are forcing a healthier diet onto people. To side-step accusations of Big Brother-style interventions, they emphasize their role as mere facilitators, encouraging individuals to make the 'right choices'. As Nikolas Rose has put it, they try to make the citizen into an 'active partner in the drive for health, accepting their responsibility for securing their own well being'.[43]

Exhorting people to become more responsible also implies that, in the past, they lacked self-control, willpower and discipline. Or to put this another way, it implies they have been acting like children. And this is the infantilizing feature that we find in many of these dietary interventions. Think about the Google employees being tricked into feeling like they were on a luxury cruise, the Danish employee in fat therapy being asked to imagine where in his body his will-power is, or the Scania employees required to attend 'health schools'.

In the great majority of cases, diets work for a short period, and then people return to their original weight. Experiences and premonitions of failure hang over many dieters. For instance, in one study we meet an IT Officer who knows that despite being a member of a healthy eating programme he will 'have a burger for lunch'. But he reassures the researcher that he has learnt something from the course: 'Now I'll eat healthier burgers from Burger King.'[44] Much of the public handwringing about the 'obesity epidemic' seems to work in a similar way. It 'produces more anxiety about obesity but fails to eradicate the behaviors that it attempts to educate people about'.[45]

Such continual failure reminds us that diets are not just sources of pleasure, joy and self-fulfilment. They are also wells of darker emotions like guilt. Gloria Sternhell notes that 'when I hear people talking about temptation, sin, guilt and shame I know they are talking about food rather than sex.'[46] To get rid of these persistent emotions of guilt we turn to ardent self-management. For instance, the author of the *5:2 Diet Book*, Kate Harrison, describes how she has suffered 'break-ups, redundancies, bereavements, money worries – and a biscuit or half a packet of biscuits is the cheapest way of making yourself feel better'. But she cautions, 'as long as you are in that comfort eating and guilt cycle, which so many of us are, there is nothing healthy about it. You are just eating because you feel grotty and then you feel you have failed again.'[47] By fasting two days a week, she was able 'to go without feeling guilt'. Dieting for her is not only about weight loss and better health. It is also about relieving guilt.

But as Zygmunt Bauman points out, dieting may also have the opposite effect, stoking rather than assuaging guilt. The implicit message of most diets, Bauman goes on to argue, is that 'you owe your body thought and care, and if you neglect that duty you should feel guilty and ashamed. Imperfections of your body are your guilt and your shame. But the redemption of sins is in the hands of the sinner, and in his or her hands alone.'[48] The link between dieting and guilt has been identified in a number of studies. One respondent explained that 'as soon as I eat something that is not on my diet, I do feel guilty, I feel really bad.'[49] This kind of state is not surprising given that one Dutch study found that 33 per cent of those participating in dietary programmes actually felt more guilty afterwards.[50] People who closely monitored their diets reported higher levels of guilt than the general population.[51] And apart from interpersonal relationships, diets were one of the most widely reported sources of guilt.[52]

That dieting triggers feelings of guilt would come as no surprise to Freud. In *Civilization and Its Discontents*, he points out that guilt arises from the superego violently admonishing the ego's plans and wishes. Sometimes, the superego might take the form of an actual person (the boss or the diet coach, for instance). But most of the time, we internalize these authority figures. When this happens 'the super-ego torments the sinful ego with the same feelings of anxiety and is on the watch for opportunities of getting it punished by the external world.'[53]The great tragedy here is that 'renunciation now no longer has a completely liberating effect; virtuous continence is no longer rewarded with the assurance of love. A threatened external unhappiness – loss of love and punishment on the part of the external authority – has been exchanged for a permanent internal unhappiness, for the tension of the sense of guilt.'[54]When you internalize the authority of the superego, you might lose a boss (or diet coach), but you gain a sense of inescapable guilt. What is more, this internal boss is exceptionally aggressive. We might hate the authority figure which demeans us by asking prying questions about personal habits; but we hate ourselves more.

If guilt was only a source of painful turmoil, we would quickly grow tired of it. But the reason why guilt is so persistent is that it also offers a sense of enjoyment. Jason Glynos points out how procrastination and smoking torment him with a sense of guilt, but at the same time give him a sense of satisfaction.[55] He is also aware that the enjoyment he takes from these moments of transgression only bind him closer to the morals of work and wellness.

These are not just individual experiences. Guilt can be a social experience. Glynos talks about heading out to the field to smoke with colleagues. When sucking down the carcinogens, this group of clandestine smokers are not just bound together by the descending gloom of provincial England or shared workplace gossip. They are also held together by their shared transgressions. The small communal relief from the first drag on the cigarette is not just the nicotine kick. It is a collective kick of violating the wellness ethic. By indulging in a common guilty habit, they develop a sense of common identity. It is what Pascal Bruckner has called a masochistic identity – a sense of collective self always looking for reaffirmation through punishment.[56] For such groups, it is only through collective punishment that a sense of solidarity is achieved. The same goes for the community of dieters who are bound together not just through the kilograms they have shed, but also through how they violated the rules of their diet. It is these collective and often hidden transgressions and sense of guilt that a community of dieters share – but they are also what tie them closer to that which they seek to resist.

Following the Daniel Plan, the 5:2 diet or any other diet, for that matter, is not simply a matter of rational self-preservation, self-creation or conformity with the norms of what Philip Mirowski calls 'everyday neo-liberalism'.[57] There are also murky reasons why many millions of dieters voluntarily commit themselves to something that they know they won't follow through and might actually make them fatter. Far from getting rid of a sense of guilt, dieting actually perpetuates it. While unmistakably unpleasant, guilt can add a degree of allure to boring everyday experiences. It is no surprise that the overweight are often so attached to dieting – the inevitable violation makes their chosen vice even more enjoyable. Furthermore, dieting offers the 'added extra' of binding people together through a shared sense of guilt and violation. In societies where everything has become permissible and social bonds are increasingly brittle, one way to inject a touch of risky pleasure into an everyday experience and placate your loneliness is to go on a diet.

Guilt plays an especially important part not just in dieting, but in the wellness syndrome more generally. The command to be healthy often comes with a not so subtle underlying message: if you don't shackle yourself to a diet, carefully monitor your weight and seek to get back to some kind of imagined original state (whether that be Palaeolithic life, biblical times or the garden of Eden), then you are a morally defiled person. Even if you do start on a dieter's journey, then you are likely to come up short. The end result, of course, is a lingering sense of guilt about your inevitable slip-ups. But what is more, this guilt becomes seductive. It not only binds us to fellow guilty parties, it is also binding us ever more tightly to the wellness syndrome.

Guilt might come with hidden benefits, but such feelings are difficult to maintain – particularly when there is a strong demand to be upbeat and self-assertive. One way of dealing with our inevitable failures to live up to the wellness command, and the uncomfortable guilt this entails, is to project it onto others. A convenient figure to this end, as we will now see, is a recently emerging figure known as the chav – an acronym interchangeably standing for Council House And Violent, or Council House And Vulgar.

'The Lower Classes Smell'

When Vicky Pollard appeared on the popular television series *Little Britain*, she was an instantly recognizable figure to the UK audience. She embodied a well-known cultural trope in the British vernacular – the overweight, oversexed and out-of-control working-class girl/woman in a tracksuit who is a menace to public safety, civil order and, above all, middle-class aesthetics and morality.

Writing in *The Times*, James Delingpole argued that 'the reason Vicky Pollard caught the public imagination is that she embodies with such fearful accuracy several of the great scourges of contemporary Britain: aggressive all-female gangs of embittered, hormonal, drunken teenagers; gym slip mums who choose to get pregnant as a career option; pasty-faced, lard-gutted slappers who'll drop their knickers in the blink of an eye.'[58] Delingpole assures us that 'these people do exist and are every bit as ripe and just a target for social satire as were, say, the raddled working-class drunks sent up by Hogarth in Gin Lane.'

The Pollard character did not get such a warm reception from all quarters. Reacting to Delingpole's claim, Owen Jones argued that 'Pollard is, of course, a grotesque carica-ture of a white working-class mum invented by two wealthy, privately educated men.'[59] In his book *Chavs: The Demoni-zation of the Working Class*, Jones argues that the Pollard character is by no means a one-off.[60] Rather, she is but one example of a giant catalogue of negative representations of working-class people, in which they are defined as irrespon-sible, feckless and overly promiscuous.

One forum in which this image can be routinely found is on reality television shows, where working-class women are portrayed binge drinking, wearing inappropriate clothes, fighting and having sex in public. In her analysis of this phenomenon, Bev Skeggs has pointed out how working-class women are represented in the mainstream national media as being 'beyond governance'.[61] They are 'anarchy on stilts', to use Germane Greer's words.[62] They are excessively loud, boisterous, foul-mouthed and, of course, drunk. But more than that, they have lost control over their bodies. Skeggs reminds us of the expanding genre of 'fat programmes', such as *Health of the Nation*, *You Are What You Eat*, *The Biggest Loser*, *Supersize vs Superskinny* and *Embarrassing Bodies*. Superficially, these shows are set up as dietary interventions by trim health professionals trying to help the overweight change their habits, mend their health, transform the way others look at them, and, most importantly, how they look at themselves. The message is familiar: by regaining self-control over one's life, it is possible to win back a sense of self-esteem.

Although fat television presents a resolutely self-empowered face to the outside world, Skeggs points to a barely hidden undercurrent. For her, such shows aim to 'expose working-class families, especially mothers, as incapable of knowing how to look after themselves and others, as irresponsible'.[63] Fat shows visualize 'the failures of self-responsibility. They provide a spectacle of subjectivity turned sour, an epidemic of the will, their own responsibility for making bad choices.'[64] These exhibitions remind the viewer what it means to be irresponsible and have a body which is undisciplined. Fat shows are not really meant to be instructional devices for working-class people. Rather, they are designed for middle-class audiences, who seamlessly alternate between feelings of moralization and disgust, on the one hand, and sadistic amusement, on the other.

In an age where jokes targeted at 'women' and 'minorities' have become socially unacceptable, one of the few terrains still available for the discriminating comic is the overweight. For sure, the fat man has always been funny. But what is striking with today's comic fat man is that we laugh not simply at his heft, but at his inept lifestyle choices. A popular English comic duo works with this theme: Lee Nelson stands on stage and delivers gags about the day-to-day life of an underclass chav. The most crucial part of this performance is not the upbeat tales of teen parentage and welfare scams, but the role played by his side-kick, the overweight chav Omelette. The main comic contribution of this character is to sit on stage, grin and eat snack foods during the entire performance.

The image of the overweight chav has made its way from popular culture into politics. The Conservative Parliamentary Under-Secretary of State for Health, Anna Soubry, told *The Daily Telegraph* 'the most deprived children at school used to be known as "skinny runts" in the past because they were malnourished.'[65] In a familiar turn, she points out that it is '"deeply ironic" that children now suffer because their parents supply them with "an abundance of bad food,"' then adding: 'It is a heartbreaking fact that people who are some of the most deprived in our society are living on an inadequate diet. But this time it's an abundance of bad food.' According to Soubry, these people don't know how to eat properly. And worse, they don't know how to structure their lives. As she remarks, 'there are houses where they don't any longer have dining tables. They will sit in front of the telly and eat.'

A consistent theme in these representations of chavs is the excesses of food, drink, sex and bling. These habits appear as if they were a matter of personal choice or family norms, making 'chav behaviour' a target for moral judgement. We are encouraged to look at just how fat, unhealthy, drunk, rude and poorly dressed characters like Vicky Pollard are. It is their very physical degradation – and the implied inability to 'look after themselves' – that our attention is drawn to. These judgements are primarily formed on one basis – disgust. Imogen Tyler argues that what the middle-class viewer finds so funny about Vicky Pollard is that she drinks, uses foul language and smokes.[66] If this is not enough, to the same viewer's delightful disgust, she pisses in a public swimming pool.

These emotions of disgust have become the basis for assessing public behaviour, cultural tastes, child rearing, clothing choice, sexual behaviour and diet. The language of disgust informs how the British middle classes talk about the working class. In *The Road to Wigan Pier*, George Orwell points out

the real secret of class distinctions in the West – the real reason why a European of bourgeois upbringing, even when he calls himself a Communist, cannot without a hard effort think of a working man as his equal. It is summed up in four

frightful words which people nowadays are chary of utter-
ing, but which were bandied about quite freely in my childhood. The words were: *The lower classes smell.*[67]

Stephanie Lawler points out that for middle-class people
'their very selves are produced in opposition to "the low"
and the low cannot do anything but repulse them'.[68] These
feelings of disgust come when the judging gaze is directed at
the working class. The focus of judgement is not their occupation, income, education or any other indicator that professional poverty trackers may be interested in. Instead, it is
food, drink, fat, clothes and fucking. Lawler points out that
by feeling disgusted about these things, and, crucially, com-
municating this disgust, middle-class people seek to distinguish themselves from the 'disgusting' working classes.

Being disgusted entails judging from the gut. In place of
cool reason, or even heated emotion, disgust works with
bodily reactions. To say someone is disgusting is to say that
they 'turn your stomach'. Such judgements are based purely
on bodily and physical sensation. Indeed, David Hume recognized this when he pointed out that many moral judgements have their basis in sentiment rather than reason. He
famously wrote that 'reason is, and ought only to be the slave
of the passions, and can never pretend to any other office
than to serve and obey them.'[69] Expanding on Hume, the
moral psychologist Jonathan Haidt argues that when we are
faced with a moral problem, we tend to rapidly make what
he calls a 'gut judgement'.[70] Only later do we build a sense
of rational justification. Haidt and his collaborators demonstrate this through a series of colourful experiments where
subjects (usually their students) are asked to make moral
assessments about scenarios which are designed to evoke
gut reactions, but do not involve any harm. Here is one
example: 'A man goes to the supermarket once a week and
buys a dead chicken. But before cooking the chicken, he has
sexual intercourse with it. Then he cooks it and eats it.'[71]
When asked about these scenarios, most subjects made snap

moral judgements and proclaimed them abhorrent. When asked why this was the case, they struggled to find rational explanations. These experiments led Haidt and his team to propose that bodily emotions such as disgust are the original inhabitants of our moral imagination. Reason is only an interloper that arrives later on the scene. This makes it difficult to contest these snap judgements.

Whether it has a primordial basis or not, the sensation of disgust taps into what Ange-Marie Hancock calls 'the politics of disgust'.[72] Looking at President Clinton's welfare reforms in the mid-1990s, she notes how a new figure arrived on the public stage – the Welfare Queen. She was a single mother, usually a woman of colour, who had multiple children, and harvested income from the welfare system. The Welfare Queen is the transatlantic cousin of the chavette. And like the chavette, she has been routinely branded as 'disgusting'. When disgust enters into politics, democratic deliberation is replaced by vitriolic monologue. We come to assume that a set of typical (disgusting) characteristics apply to all figures in the same category. Any kind of solidarity we may have felt now disappears, and we no longer want to talk to the figure branded as disgusting, let alone touch them.

When we react to something or someone with a sense of disgust, then the door is open to overly hasty moral judgements. It should therefore come as no surprise that judgements of disgust are deeply related to morality. Many years ago, the anthropologist Mary Douglas noted how, across many cultures, dirt and uncleanliness were often deeply connected with moral defilement.[73] For instance, many religions banned some foods, people or activities because they were seen as being dirty, dangerous but also morally debased. This suggests that judgements of disgust have a moral basis. When we say that we are disgusted by someone's clothes, habits or food, we are also implying that they are morally defiled.

The figure of the chav is convenient as chavs embody the life that the perfect human shuns. They embody the flip side of everything the wellness lover is. They are unfit, overweight, unpleasant, unmindful of others and have a distinctively negative attitude. But they are also a convenient repository for much of the guilt which those trapped in the wellness syndrome suffer from. If the wo/man of now misses an early morning spinning class, s/he can get a little relief by turning on the television, watching *Embarrassing Bodies* and thinking 'at least I don't look like *that*'.

Being disgusted by overweight chavs might temporarily relieve the wo/man of now's sense of guilt. But it also sits uncomfortably with this wo/man's need to be a caring, conscious and socially concerned individual. To head off this potential contradiction, some biomoralists seek to 'reach out' from their own perfectly constructed world. Reviving the spirit of nineteenth-century philanthropists, they want to save the degraded and disgusting. But how can they do this? Provide them with improved housing? A basic income? Health care? No. The answer seems to be this: teach them how to cook an organic vegetable bake.

How Focaccia Saved Britain

One of the most popular television documentary genres during the first decade of the twenty-first century, at least in the United Kingdom, was the cooking show. Each cooking show provided a kind of ideal subject position. There was Nigella Lawson for the slightly overweight middle-class housewife who wanted to think of her increasing girth as sexy curves; Rick Stein, who allowed the bored middle-aged man to imagine his trip to the local up-scale supermarket as a visit to an exotic fishing village in the Mediterranean; Hugh Fearnley-Whittingstall for the frustrated teacher imagining a rural life while preparing a meal for uninteresting acquaintances on Saturday night; Gordon Ramsay for the office sadist who takes his anger out on a side of beef after work. And of course there was Jamie Oliver.

What makes Jamie Oliver of particular interest to the critic of postmodern ideology is not his astounding success, his impressive multimedia business empire or his canny ability to meld the mores of middle-class cookery with a kind of light working-class linguistic toolkit. Rather, it is his ability to perform a series of striking conjuring acts which transformed an organic focaccia from an item in the River Café (an overpriced Italian restaurant which overlooks the Thames in London) into an expression of laddish masculinity (something one might roll out between reading a soft porn magazine and watching football), into a way of creating an authentic connection with one's alienated family (by making it over a fire during a camping trip), and finally into something which might save the neglected children in deprived communities across the world. Jamie Oliver's importance in the history of British cookery is not due to his skill, his questionable charms or even his taste in shirts. Rather he is one of its most important figures because he has transformed food into a kind of moral intervention designed to correct nearly any social and personal ill. He has been the prime champion of what has become a widespread contemporary doxa: eating well can make you into a morally good person – even against your own will.

Perhaps the most striking example of Jamie's genius – and which made him a pioneering figure for culinary ideology – was his ground-breaking show *Jamie's School Dinners*. In this well-known series Jamie sought to reform the lives of children in a rather deprived school by changing the food which they were served during their lunchtime in the school canteen. The series started out with the usual parade of shocking facts about the massive increases in childhood obesity: the widespread inactivity of the young, the amount of fat and sugar consumed, and the serious long-term health risks which this poses. This epidemiological abstract was made somewhat more concrete when we were introduced to the rancid food which the inmates of this culinary prison were forced to eat. This included a rather alarming item called the Turkey Twizzler (a kind of popsicle-shaped meat product of unidentifiable origins). After setting the scene,

Jamie launched his campaign to transform the lives of the school children by changing the menu in a South London school. Out went burgers and fries, in came vegetable bake. To add drama to this tale, our good chef and his team quickly faced rebellion from overworked staff in the canteen, children who preferred the unhealthy food they were used to, and their parents, who felt so sorry for their offspring they were willing to deliver high-fat food (like chips) to the school.

Like all good heroes, Mr Oliver was able to overcome this opposition by getting the staff on his side, educating children in skills such as naming a vegetable, encouraging students to sample his food, and informing parents of the benefits of healthy eating. The result was framed as a triumph not just in this school, but in schools throughout the country. Over 250,000 outraged citizens mobilized to produce a petition calling for better food to be served in school canteens. National politicians such as Tony Blair took notice and made some cordial pledges, saying that all children should have healthy meals at school. But there were some more concrete advances, too. Particularly bedevilled food items such as the Turkey Twizzler and soft drinks were banned by some local authorities. The national government also devoted £60 million to establishing a School Food Trust. These results, coupled with changes in public discourse about food in schools, led many to assume that through the humble focaccia, Jamie had launched a 'food revolution'.

Never to miss an opportunity for publicity, Mr Oliver continued his 'food revolution' in a series of follow-up television shows. In the first, he returned to the school where it all started. He found some concerning signs that many of his gastronomic reforms were failing to take hold. The school canteen carrying his menu was losing money and the students were returning to school with various junk food items. To address these issues, Oliver launched a range of initiatives, including a Junk Amnesty, where children were asked to hand in unhealthy food items as if they were handguns. Never to be dismayed, Oliver launched a campaign to take his 'food revolution' further – to schools in Lincolnshire, where he convinced local pubs and restaurants to use their kitchens to prepare food for nearby schools.

In a later series, Jamie extended his food crusading to Rotherham in South Yorkshire. This particular location was selected because it had been identified as the obesity capital of the United Kingdom. It was also home to one of the great reactionaries against his food revolution – Julie Critchlow. Ms Critchlow gained brief exposure in the global media when she was recorded mounting an effort to resist one of Mr Oliver's culinary movements by passing burgers, chips and crisps through the fence of a comprehensive school to her children. When accused of feeding her children a diet that condemned them to obesity, Ms Critchlow responded by pointing out: 'We know what food the kids like, and it's not polenta.'[74] As her acts of resistance against Jamie's attempts to change food in schools became widely known, she came to be a kind of anti-biomoral icon. To deal with this backlash, Mr Oliver began by meeting a single mother of two young children called Natasha. She was selected presumably because she had little in the way of knowledge about cooking. During the visit she showed the camera a fridge filled with junk food. This led Jamie to beat a rapid retreat to his Land Rover, where he despaired: 'Fucking hell...it's fucking Great Britain. It's 2008. I've been to Soweto and I've seen AIDS orphans eating better than this.' This shock experience sent Mr Oliver into yet another round of revolutionary activities – this time through teaching adults with little or no culinary knowledge some basic skills (which he encouraged them to pass on). He established a Ministry of Food which aimed to reach out to members of the community and school them in the arts of cooking. The name, which harked back to the Ministry of Food established during World War Two, framed the initiative in one of the favourite ideological motifs of British culture – the supposed human flourishing and solidarity amid the depravations of the war. While making progress, Oliver also faced some resistance, including an entire football crowd at the local pitch mocking his food moralizing by singing football chants such as 'Who Ate All the Pies?' Although many locals remained unconvinced about this 'food revolution', sixteen local councils throughout the United Kingdom supported the initiative, and five Ministry of Food centres were opened, some of which now face uncertain futures.

Throughout these television series, we encounter all of the components of biomorality. We are encouraged to be disgusted by what people eat. In the Ministry of Food, the viewer's moral outrage is whipped up by showing how the citizens of Rotherham are 'unable to read recipes, use a stove, mash a potato', and don't 'know what boiling water looks like', or even how to 'feed their own children'.[75] While the class dimension is constantly in our face, the issues are nevertheless repackaged as matters of 'lifestyle'. We are reminded that eating chips and curry sauce every evening is not only an affront to health, but a sign of the wider state of moral decline within broken Britain. Finally, we are entreated that individuals should take responsibility for their own health and wellbeing – in this case, with a little help from a friendly celebrity chef. Using the methods of reality television, the show sought to 'bring less educated, lower income populations up to middle class standards'.[76] The implicit message seems to be that in order to address a serious social problem we should not call for state interventions, because that would just create more problems. What is needed instead is what some have called 'moral entrepreneurship', whereby an inspirational figure seeks to transform individuals and inspire them to take responsibility for their own health through eating correctly.[77]

What is so striking about this food crusade is not Jamie Oliver's ability to establish a strange kind of biomoral panopticon where each failure to consume the correct number of vegetable portions is presented to millions.[78] Rather, it is the audacious assumption that serious social policy issues (the educational fate of poor children in the United Kingdom) can be addressed through a spectacular dietary intervention. Underlying *Jamie's School Dinners* – and indeed the range of social crusading food shows which have appeared in its wake – is the belief that a set of broad social and economic issues can be put aside in favour of a simple bodily intervention through food. The assumption in *Jamie's School Dinners* is that the fate of these children is not so much determined by broader government education policy, by deeply entrenched class structures in British society, by systemic unemployment, or even by the vagaries of global capitalism. Rather, the fate of these children is determined by the food they put into their mouths. In this sense the Turkey Twizzler becomes a horrific object not because of its unclear content, its distasteful colour or the glistening sheen of the grease in which it is covered. Rather, the viewer finds it so disgusting because this meat-popsicle stands in for all forms of discrimination, injustices and humiliations which are routinely visited on school children now and indeed for the rest of their lives.

Why did *Jamie's School Dinners* strike such a widespread chord? Probably because it keyed into the assumption that political interventions – let alone broader political ideologies – are only useful and acceptable when they assiduously avoid broader issues (such as the welfare state) and instead focus on increasingly narrow behavioural interventions. Questions about government services, industry policy, gender roles or the broader British class system are off the agenda. The only palatable form which political action comes in is a menu change and a few cooking classes. The kind of pathos which so often leads middle-class reformers like Jamie Oliver to suddenly recognize the suffering of the world and declare that 'something must be done' is channelled into ever narrower furrows. While this effectively leaves many of the broader – and arguably more vital – issues of true political importance off the table, it allows the incensed middle-class activist to think that he or she has have indeed done something worthy and concrete.

Such is the logic of biomorality: it gives a sense of smug righteousness, making you think you're on the right side of the moral law. If only people would be more like you – or more like Jamie Oliver – the world would be a much better place. Not just a happier place, but a healthier place too.

3

The Happiness Doctrine

What do we do now, now that we are happy?
Samuel Beckett, *Waiting for Godot*, 1953[1]

How to be Really Truly Happy

'I feel that life is divided into the horrible and the miserable,'
Woody Allen's nervous and fast-talking character tells his
girlfriend Annie Hall while browsing through a bookshop
in search of new titles about death. Among the horrible,
Allen goes on to explain, we find the terminal cases, blind
people, the crippled. 'And the miserable is everyone else,' he
continues. 'So you should be thankful that you're miserable,
because that's very lucky, to be miserable.'

Martin Seligman, the high priest of positive psychology,
would not consider himself lucky to be miserable. For him,
Freudian modesty is overrated. Turning hysterical misery
into common unhappiness is simply not an achievement. For
Seligman, the question is this: 'How to go from plus two to
plus seven in your life, not just how to go from minus five
to minus three.'[2] There is no need to go into the actual
numbers and to ponder whether they are based on scientific

evidence or improvised on the spot. (We will have reasons to come back to the 'scientific' basis of happiness studies.) Seligman sees happiness rather like a gigantic hi-fi that can be turned up, and made louder and richer. All you need to do is to put your mind to it. As the motivational guru Zig Ziglar has put it: 'I'm super good, but I'll get better.'[3]

After being elected President of the American Psychological Association in 1997, Seligman made positive psychology the theme of his candidacy. This implied a new orientation towards the positive side of psychology, as opposed to the negative dimension that he viewed as an unfortunate legacy of the depressive days of Freud. Why not focus on the positive side, and find out recipes that could benefit the whole population? And so Seligman and his associates managed to initiate a movement that would combine the $10 billion self-improvement industry with what Goldacre has labelled bad science[4] and a simplified version of Bentham's greatest-happiness-of-the-greatest-number slogan.

But positive psychology – or, more precisely, positive thinking – did not begin with Seligman. It has a long history, which the journalist Barbara Ehrenreich, in her book *Smile or Die*,[5] traces back to Calvinism. This religion, although diverse, emphasized self-examination and hard work. It did not have a positive, upbeat tone. It is better described, Ehrenreich suggests, as 'socially imposed depression'.[6] This religion seemed perfectly suited to the harsh times of the eighteenth and nineteenth centuries in America. But as better times loomed in the mid-1800s, Calvinism would gradually lose its popularity. At around this time, in the 1860s, a new movement began to take hold. This was the New Thought movement, which presented a strange mix of Emersonian nature-worship, Swedenborgian mysticism and a pinch of Hinduism. In contrast with Calvinism, this movement saw humans as divine creatures equipped with infinitely powerful minds. Using these powers in the right way could help humans overcome any difficulties in life, including physical illness.

So as we move into the latter part of the nineteenth century, Calvinism has become regarded as an enemy, accused of being a source of illness. Even so, we can still discern some features of Calvinism. As Ehrenreich notes, positive thinking 'ended up preserving some of Calvinism's more toxic features – a harsh judgmentalism, echoing the religion's condemnation of sin, and an insistence on the constant interior labor of self-examination'.[7] This is the essence of positive thinking: it combines magical thinking (you can achieve anything with a positive attitude) with a harsh insistence on personal responsibility (if you fail, it's your fault).

Positive thinking was brought to the masses in 1952 with the publication of Norman Vincent Peale's *The Power of Positive Thinking.*[8] Strongly influenced by the New Thought movement, Peale, a Methodist minister turned Protestant pastor, presented a new evangelical message of how to win back your self-confidence. In the book, Peale offered a practical guide, based on what he knew about Christianity and New Thought, which would help ordinary people overcome the ordeals of everyday life. While his message would appeal to a wide range of people, it was perfectly designed for the lonely salesman who suffered from declining self-esteem and was in urgent need of a confidence boost. In the opening pages of the book Peale recounts a story of a salesman on the edge of a nervous breakdown who desperately turns to him for advice. The salesman is just about to make a deal of life-and-death importance, and Peale asks him to calm down. He then gives the salesman a few confidence-boosting words to repeat, over and over again, until he regains his composure. Peale succeeds, of course, and does not fail to take credit. In his defence, he is not writing in a genre defined by modesty.

Sentimental anecdotes and words of wisdom are used to persuade the readers about the extraordinary things you can do with your mind. According to this genre, your entire life is shaped by your attitude. The job for Peale and others is to give some guidance to the reader. Peale writes in the beginning of *The Power of Positive Thinking*: 'The system outlined is a perfect and amazing method of successful living.'[9] Again, he is not in the business of making modest claims.

A crucial component of positive thinking is the promise of success. It talks directly to the dream of catapulting yourself into a prominent position in American society, replete with extraordinary wealth and a large fenced garden. This focus on success had a central place in the first generation of self-help books, from Dale Carnegie's *How to Win Friends and Influence People* (1936) to Napoleon Hill's *Think and Grow Rich* (1937).

The classic narrative of these books typically involves a person who is struggling through life with the odds against him. With the aid of positive thinking, this struggler pulls himself up by his own bootstraps. An exemplar of this genre is the soap salesman S.B. Fuller, whose story we are told in the best-seller *Success Through a Positive Mental Attitude*,[10] one of Napoleon Hill's later books (co-authored with W. Clement Stone). One day, S.B. Fuller 'began to *want* to be rich'. He focused his mind on the things he wanted and, by fully integrating that mental model into his life, he reached a point where wealth and success finally came to him. 'Now the important thing to notice here is that S.B. Fuller started life with fewer advantages than most of us have,'[11] Hill and Stone tell the reader, hence suggesting that *you too* can be S.B. Fuller and turn your life around and become rich (or successful by other means).

Success and happiness often appear shoulder-to-shoulder. This suggests that happiness opens up an infinite array of possibilities: to meet new friends, become rich, develop a closer relationship to oneself. In *Waiting for Godot* Vladimir tells Estragon to say he is happy, 'even if it's not true'. Estragon finally grants his friend's request, saying that he is happy, then adding: 'What do we do now, now that we are happy?' While for Beckett it is questionable whether happiness would lead to anything at all, the proponents of positive thinking would argue that it is the key to everything good in life. It all begins with happiness. The early twentieth-century theologian Albert Schweitzer is often quoted in self-help manuals for saying: 'Success is not the key to happiness. Happiness is the key to success.' But this assumption is not restricted to pop psychology and self-help. Many academics subscribe to the belief that happiness and psychological wellbeing 'are linked to higher levels of income, more successful marriages and friendship and better health and... better work performance'.[12] Some have objected to this causal explanation by raising the question that it might be the other way round: that high income in a society where money is regarded as important would make people feel happier, or at least prevent them from being unhappy insofar as they can pay their rent and put food on the table. But positive thinking, and its multitude of self-help cousins, insists that success begins with happiness. That is the basic philosophical premise. The mind is more forceful than material conditions. It is happiness (over which we are assumed to have more control) that conditions our living standard and whether or not we have a job.

While the doctrine suggesting that happiness is the key to a prosperous and successful life stands unchallenged, there are varying views of what happiness is. For Peale and his acolytes, mainly talking to lonely salesmen and others struggling to make ends meet, the crucial question was how they could boost their confidence to achieve things – whether to prevent their wives from leaving them or to successfully close the next business deal. If the smile was fake, then so be it. It works, and that's all that matters. In an age where image plays a crucial role, there is simply no time for trying to distinguish the real from the fake. As Ziglar advises, 'When your image improves, your performance improves.'[13]

Meanwhile, for someone like Deepak Chopra, whose work may appeal more to the unhappy housewife longing for a deeper spiritual experience, the real issue is not about improving your image but finding your real, authentic, self.

'The true self lies beyond images,' he writes. 'It can be found at a level of existence that is independent of the good and bad opinions of others.'[14] Real happiness, then, needs to be carefully separated from the fake version, based on a blind and selfish quest to become rich and famous. In *The Happiness Trap*,[15] Russ Harriss argues that we have been guided by a misconception of what happiness really is. We have been running after the wrong thing, for a long time, and that has caused considerable unhappiness. But this can be rectified, he reassuringly explains. Just try his new revolutionary therapy – Acceptance and Commitment Therapy – and you will be able to live not just happily but mindfully, in peace with yourself and others.

This has become a dominant theme in the self-help genre. All previous books have misunderstood the true meaning of happiness. They are too superficial. Even society has misunderstood what happiness is. Real happiness cannot be found in the external world by following the codes handed to us by society. As Nicola Phoenix writes in *Reclaiming Happiness*, 'the external things that we're trying so desperately to obtain are only transitory.'[16] Instead we need to look inwards and find a more sustainable form of happiness that goes beyond the social norms of a big car and a beautiful house. Even consumerism and commercialism – the backbone of American society – have been questioned by this subgenre. Phoenix writes that 'over-consumption at least shows us that having more doesn't make us happy.'[17] And Thomas Bien, in *The Buddha's Way of Happiness*, critically reflects on a Coca-Cola advertisement with the caption 'Open Happiness', claiming that the 'idea that some product will make us happy doesn't survive even cursory examination'.[18] But this authentic orientation to happiness, which emphasizes its inward nature, has something crucial in common with the happiness promoted by Norman Vincent Peale: that happiness, when it comes down to it, is a choice. Happiness is an orientation to the world, and, since it is *your* orientation, *you* can change it. Listen to Veronica Ray and her book

Choosing Happiness. She begins by describing happiness as a spiritual state of mind, devoid of antagonism: 'Happiness is a feeling inside us that everything is all right. It is the absence of fear, confusion, and conflict. It is a place of rest, contentment, and joy. It is peace of mind.' Then comes the crucial line: 'The most important thing to learn about happiness, I believe, is that it is a *choice*. We always have it available to us; it's within each of us.'[19]

Martin Seligman is a direct successor of Norman Vincent Peale. He promotes the same individuality gospel: happiness (and hence success) is a choice that the individual can make, even when the material conditions seem to suggest otherwise. And yet, Seligman is careful to distance himself from Peale and others from that generation. Happiness is a sacred territory for Seligman, which needs to be protected from false prophets; and to him, Peale is just a cheap happiness-monger. Seligman sees himself, and his method, as the real thing. It is based, he often emphasizes, on science, contrary to positive thinking, which is based on a series of illusory anecdotes designed to help the desperate regain their confidence. 'It is important to see the difference between this approach and the so-called power of positive thinking,' Seligman writes in his 2003 best-seller *Authentic Happiness*: 'Positive thinking often involves trying to believe upbeat statements such as ' "Every day, in every way, I'm getting better and better" ' in the absence of evidence, or even in the face of contrary evidence....Many educated people, trained in skeptical thinking, cannot manage this kind of boosterism.'[20]

If Peale wrote for the lonely salesman to help him get through the day, Seligman writes for the educated classes to help them distinguish their real sense of happiness from other people's false sense of happiness. And this is a crucial dimension of happiness studies, to demonstrate how their version of happiness – or their version of a good life – is more authentic than others. In *Against Happiness*, Eric G. Wilson, a professor of English, levels a scathing attack on the happiness industry and its demand that we all ought to be happy. For him, technology has destroyed our interpersonal relationship; Prozac and Paxil have destroyed our emotional awareness; our cities have been transformed into massive shopping malls; and politics has been reduced to cheap entertainment. And it is our obsession with this superficial quest for happiness that, more than anything else, has destroyed our relationship to what is real. Wilson does not bother much to conceal his contempt for happiness-seekers. 'These dreams are ultimately delusional, and narcissistically so,' he writes. 'They colonize experience. They impose their imperialist egos onto the world. They reduce difference to the same.'[21] These people, whom Wilson regards as alien and inferior, are ultimately bad people because they do not know how to live according to the principles of what he regards as a meaningful life. 'That's finally it,' Wilson concludes, 'happy types ultimately don't live their own lives at all.'[22]

Wilson would not be happy to be compared to Seligman. He is a respected professor of English who makes sure to mention his Proust collection and writes sentimentally (although not very perceptively) about Blake, Dickinson, Coleridge and Keats. But Seligman would be equally hurt by a comparison with Norman Vincent Peale or Zig Ziglar. Seligman holds a respected position in a top university and is eager to show his interest in art and literature. Authentic happiness is not, he suggests, going to come to you if you look for it in 'drugs, chocolate, loveless sex, shopping, masturbation and television'.[23] Zig Ziglar does not exactly promote drugs and masturbation as a road to happiness. But watch a YouTube video of Ziglar and you will understand why Seligman wants to be dissociated.

This is also how we need to understand happiness in an age of biomorality. It is not just a moral demand that is placed on the individual. It is not enough to be outgoing, visible and flexible. One also has to integrate these features into one's persona so that they appear natural and congruous with the person you really are.

Herein lies the paradox of the happiness command. On the one hand, we are asked to change our attitudes and to employ our willpower. When we focus our attention on the positive aspects of life, good things will come our way. Happiness, here, is an individual choice, available to anyone who is open to change his or her attitude. On the other hand, we are told that we cannot fool ourselves and just pretend to be happy. Happiness is a deep emotion which does not come to us easily, at least not the real kind of happiness. To achieve authentic happiness is not for everyone. It requires that you change your entire person, stop eating chocolate and masturbating, and instead spend more time at the museum. If happiness is still a choice here, it is not a choice for all of us.

The Bad Science of Happiness

Positive psychology is not at all like positive thinking, Seligman declares. First of all, his version of happiness is more profound. A happy life, for Seligman, involves going to the museum and looking at Monet's *Water Lilies*; staying at home and reading sentimental prose; taking long walks in the forest and listening to bird song. He promotes a sustainable and authentic form of happiness, which, for him, has nothing in common with the fast and saturated happiness that is sold in packages.

For Seligman, happiness is not just authentic. It is also scientific. When he launched his positive psychology campaign in 1997, he faced a difficult challenge: how to persuade the academic community that his notion of happiness had scientific legitimacy and that it was a subject worthy of academic inquiry. One of the greatest hurdles for Seligman was to convince his academic colleagues that positive psychology was not normative pop psychology. Its basic premise – that a positive attitude will lead to great things – did suggest a slightly normative twist, but Seligman found a way to work around this problem. He agrees that science must be descriptive, not prescriptive, then adds: 'It is not the job of Positive Psychology to tell you that you should be optimistic, or spiritual, or kind, or good-humored; it is rather to describe the consequences of these traits (for example, that being optimistic brings about less depression, better physical health, and higher achievement, at a cost perhaps of less realism).'[24] One might imagine a menacing and over-protective father using the same rhetoric to steer his daughter in the right direction: 'It is not my job to tell you that you should not wear short skirts, or high heels; I am just describing the consequences of doing so.'

Barbara Ehrenreich wanted to know more about the scientific basis of positive psychology. Going straight to the source, she had scheduled to meet Seligman at his office at the University of Pennsylvania. After a long wait (apparently he had some more urgent issues to resolve first), he insisted on taking her to the museum to look at Monet's *Water Lilies*. On arriving at the museum he suggested going to a public lecture about learned helplessness (one of his previous research interests), but the event was sold out.

Ehrenreich had a series of questions about Seligman's book *Authentic Happiness* ('which I had found just as elusive as he was turning out to be'[25]). She was particularly interested in the happiness equation, which she describes as 'one of the most irritatingly pseudoscientific assertions in his book'. The equation – $H = S + C + V$ – describes how one's enduring level of happiness (H) is determined by three factors: (S) your set range; (C) circumstances; and (V) things that you can change. In other words, happiness is determined by the person you are, and the circumstance you have – some of which are more amenable to change than others. Suspicious of the scientific basis of the equation, Ehrenreich asked, 'What are the units of measurements?' Seligman reluctantly explained that, 'C is going to decompose into twenty different things, like religion and marriage.'[26] Although Ehrenreich tried to tease out a more elaborate and coherent explanation from him, she could not get one. 'But clearly

Seligman wanted an equation,' Ehrenreich sums up in her reflections, 'because equations add a veneer of science.'[27]

Even if Seligman, in his interview with Ehrenreich, fails to convincingly explain the scientific rigour of his work, he has proved to be wildly successful in influencing his academic colleagues. Since the late 1990s, positive psychology has managed to dissociate itself from the legacy of positive thinking and become a sub-discipline in its own right, attracting a steady stream of external funding, introducing happiness studies to university curriculums, even having its own academic outlet, the *Journal of Happiness Studies*.

One of the academic disciplines which has shown most interest in this new field of inquiry is business studies. This is not too surprising. Business schools have always had a complicated relationship to science, and have a long tradition of repackaging ideology as academic studies. Versions of positive psychology engineered in business schools have been called into question, not just because they are based on shaky assumptions, but also because they appear to be harbingers of a vision of capitalism where exploitation and hierarchies are promoted as a common good.

This was the critical question that business schools had to address as they emerged at the dawn of the last century: how to legitimize their existence and to persuade the world that managers are good people who are vital for the wellbeing of a society. The industrial engineer Fredrick Winslow Taylor is often remembered as a pioneering scientist who helped devise new ways of making work more efficient. To this end he watched labourers loading iron. He used a stopwatch and made some rough estimations and calculations (which would make an undergraduate in statistics blush). The conclusion was not just that people could work faster and more efficiently through tighter control, but also that these factories were in urgent need of managers who would be educated enough to understand the advanced 'scientific' principles of management. This is how Taylor puts it: '[T]he science of handling pig iron is so great and amounts to so much that it is impossible for the man who is best suited to this type of work to understand the principle of this science.'[28] By giving this management method the label 'science' (even though it amounted to buying a stopwatch and making sure people work harder under tighter control), Taylor lent legitimacy to the role of managers. It became a way of justifying the manager's superior role, and keeping him at a distinctly separate level from those who were carrying out manual labour. 'From a metaphysical perspective,' Matthew Stewart surmises, 'one could say that Taylor was a "dualist": there is brain, there is brawn, and the two, he believed, very rarely meet.'[29]

Soon the Scientific Management of Taylor would run into a legitimacy crisis. It appeared needlessly harsh and dehumanizing. Enter Elton Mayo and the human relations movement, which, in the 1930s, presented a new approach to management based on the assumption that humans are not made of steel, but have emotions. The movement's point was that good managers distinguish themselves from bad ones by their ability to harness people's emotions and shape more efficient work environments. Pay recognition to your workforce and you will be paid back manifold was the new management advice that Mayo and his colleagues now began to promote. They shared Taylor's ambition to squeeze out as much energy as possible from the worker. But they thought that there are more ingenious ways to get there. Hence the birth of a new era of exploitation, one with a human face.

Since the days of Mayo, business schools have continued to subscribe to the assumption that happy workers are more productive. The assumption that happiness causes productivity (and not the other way round) is central here. Shawn Achor, for example, writes in *The Happiness Advantage*: 'Waiting to be happy limits our brain's potential for success, whereas cultivating positive brains makes us more motivated, efficient, resilient, creative, and productive, which drives performance upward.'[30] Achor then adds a

characteristic explanation: 'This discovery has been con-
firmed by thousands of scientific studies.'[31]

In an article published in the *Journal of Organizational
Behavior*, Gerald E. Ledford claims that 'the "a happy
worker is a productive worker" proposition has deep roots
in management ideology.'[32] This proposition, he continues,
'is said to obscure the legitimate grounds for conflict between
labor and management, to overemphasize social as opposed
to economic causes of poor morale, and to encourage management manipulation of employees'.[33] In other words, these
studies are repackaging an ideology promoting the individual's ultimate responsibility.

We will come back to the ideological nature of happiness
studies. But let us first point out the most obvious limitation
of these studies, namely self-reporting. People taking these
tests always have the option to report dishonestly, but the
problem cuts deeper than that. In a well-known study about
life satisfaction,[34] a team of researchers was able to demonstrate how the answers to these surveys are subject to even
the smallest changes in circumstances. Before filling in the
questionnaire, the subjects were asked to go into a separate
room to photocopy some papers where a dime had been
planted for half of the subjects. The study revealed that those
who had 'accidentally' discovered the coin reported a con-
siderably higher level of life satisfaction than the other half.

Self-reporting also raises some fundamental existential
questions, such as whether we have the same form of access
to our moods and emotions as we do to our bank accounts.
One of the basic points of psychoanalysis is that we do not
have a transparent relationship to ourselves. The unconscious makes unexpected appearances in our life. Freud's
great discovery was that we are not in full control of our
own minds. 'The ego feels uneasy,' he writes in 1917: 'It
comes up against limits to its power in its own house, the
mind.'[35] In other words, we do not have self-mastery.

When it comes to happiness, it gets more complicated still.
'Someone who is happy cannot know that he is,' Giorgio

Agamben points out, because 'the subject of happiness is not a subject per se and does not obtain the form of a consciousness.'[36] Happiness is slippery, fragile and elusive. Always on the run. It surprises us in ordinary moments, and flees when we most expect it. As Pascal Bruckner puts it: 'No one is ever sure that he is truly happy; and to ask the question is already to spoil the answer.'[37]

But these insights have not discouraged politicians from asking the question, not just to themselves, but to large parts of the population. Whether or not they spoil the answer is another matter. As we will see, they may be less interested in finding the actual answer to happiness than using this term to legitimize a particular form of politics.

Cruel Politics: When David met Martin

The meeting between Martin Seligman and Barbara Ehrenreich was disastrous, at least judged from her own description. They did not hit it off, and we can safely assume they have not stayed in touch. But some time after this meeting, Seligman was contacted by a much more significant person, the British Prime Minister, David Cameron. Unlike the annoying Ehrenreich, Cameron's intentions were genuine. He was not going to make cruel remarks about the happiness equation. He treated Seligman with the respect he thought he deserved as a highly esteemed professor and a pioneer in his field. And Cameron was armed with all of the right questions. He wanted to know if Seligman's vision of positive psychology could be successfully applied to an entire country, making it flourish without making unnecessary and expensive investments in public services.

Cameron had been fascinated by the idea of happiness for a long time and first floated the proposition of a happiness index in 2005, just after assuming leadership of the Conservative Party. But it was not until 2010 that he announced his plan to measure wellbeing in Britain. In a speech delivered in November that year, Cameron explained:

> If your goal in politics is to help make a better life for people
> – which mine is – and if you know, both in your gut and
> from a huge body of evidence that prosperity alone can't
> deliver a better life, then you've got to take practical steps
> to make sure government is properly focused on our quality
> of life as well as economic growth, and that is what we are
> trying to do.[38]

In a spirit worthy of positive psychologists, he refers to both
his gut and a huge body of evidence, knowingly failing to
specify how they relate to one another. But more interestingly, he constructs a new artificial fault line: '[P]eople are
concerned that talking about wellbeing shows that this government is somehow sidelining economic growth as our first
concern.' But Cameron comforts his audience: 'I am absolutely clear that our most urgent priority is to get the economy
moving.... We're trying to make it easier for people to start
their own business, we're cutting corporate tax, we're getting
behind entrepreneurs.'

Cameron insists that wellbeing and entrepreneurship are
not mutually exclusive – a lesson he might have learnt from
positive psychology. Wellbeing does not produce detached
hippies who will move to the forest and disappear into a
haze of magic mushrooms. On the contrary, wellbeing will
produce more responsible and hard-working people, running
on all cylinders, and only rarely in need of medical care;
because, as we will see, a positive attitude is thought to be
an effective healer.

The timing of Cameron's initiative was notable. Students
had just taken to the streets protesting over tuition fees.
Unions were mobilizing support for taking action against
planned cuts to government spending. And in the wake of
the financial crisis, the prospects for the economy looked
bleak. Initiating a nation-wide happiness survey in the midst
of a recession that was predicted to hit ordinary people hard
seemed somewhat strange, to say the least.

However, Cameron saw things differently. He did not
think of wellbeing as something that would come out of a

welfare state. If anything, he assumed that welfare restrains happiness, because it induces people to be lazy and prevents them from flourishing. Either way, these things are irrelevant. If you look at the evangelical message from positive thinking, it says that recession and austerity – indeed, almost all forms of external circumstances – have little impact on whether people regard themselves as happy or not. This is a recurring theme in happiness studies, and has been since the early 1970s.

In a well-known study from 1978, a group of psychologists wanted to understand the relative nature of happiness.[39] They used two groups. The first consisted of lottery winners who had received jackpots of between $50,000 and $1,000,000. The other group consisted of victims of serious accidents who had been paralysed (some from the waist down; others from the neck). For reference, they added a control group of 'ordinary' people who had neither won a fortune nor been paralysed. When the researchers assembled the results, they found that the lottery winners were not happier than the control group. In fact, they now took less pleasure in everyday activities. Compared to the group of newly paralysed, the lottery winners had a more pessimistic outlook on the future. From this, the researchers drew the conclusion that, in their words, 'the blind, the retarded, and the malformed are not less happy than other people.'[40]

The scientific value of self-reporting was not a source of concern for Cameron. The happiness survey that he finally launched in 2011 used a standard format, slightly simplified, but on the whole similar to those used in previous studies. Cameron's happiness survey consisted of four questions: '(1) Overall, how satisfied are you with your life nowadays?'; '(2) Overall, to what extent do you feel the things you do in your life are worthwhile?'; '(3) Overall, how happy did you feel yesterday?'; and '(4) Overall, how anxious did you feel yesterday?'[41]

One might suspect that the two last questions, asking the person how he or she was doing the previous day, were deliberately designed to prevent some cynical researchers from planting coins at the site and demonstrating, once more, the contextual sensitivity of these tests. Even so, the results did not really say much, with about 60 to 80 per cent responding that they were relatively content with things as they were. The average life-satisfaction amounted to 7.4. Critics seized the opportunity to make a few cynical remarks about the study being a waste of time and money, saying the survey was a 'statement of the bleeding obvious'.[42]

A more relevant question is not whether this survey produced an accurate account of the wellbeing of British society, or whether it failed to produce anything at all. The question is *why* Cameron would be interested in launching a happiness study in the first place. More particularly, why did he want to carry out the study at the same time as he was implementing new austerity measures? And more particularly still, why did he seek advice from Martin Seligman, whose message is that happiness is not so much to do with your circumstances as what you *do* with your circumstances?

One reading of Cameron's happiness initiative is that he wants to steer attention away from concrete sociopolitical discussions. Initiating a happiness survey takes the focus away from pressing political questions such as whether the state supports and delivers public services. But that misses the point too. What is at stake here is a more thoroughgoing reframing of the question of governance. Happiness is not a cheap compensation for the weakened welfare state. Rather it is seen as a powerful attitude that can help people to change their own situation. According to this logic, cutting benefits would not be a punishment but a necessary way to make people active. It is a policy aimed at transforming passive overweight blobs sitting on a couch watching daytime television into reformed people with a flourishing entrepreneurial spirit, running on all cylinders, with great resilience.

In this sense, the true counterpart to the neoliberal government promoting happiness is not so much Martin

Seligman as it is the Australian self-help icon Rhonda Byrne. After the first happiness survey, British newspapers began to run articles suggesting that Cameron's happiness index had failed to measure the right type of happiness. It turned out that the critique had not been levelled from the opposition. It was coming from within. As a *Guardian* article put it, 'American "optimism expert" who inspired prime minister fears that he got it all wrong.'[43] It was Martin Seligman who now distanced himself from Cameron's happiness index, raising doubts about the usefulness of these surveys. Apparently, Seligman had moved on. He had now started to doubt whether happiness was a word that one should even be talking about. 'The word "happiness" always bothered me,' he says in the article, 'partly because it was scientifically unwieldy and meant a lot of different things to different people, and also because it is subjective.'[44]

Rhonda Byrne, meanwhile, did not show any signs of reversing her position. In her best-selling book (first released as a DVD) she presents the perfect ideological complement to neoliberalism. She calls it *The Secret*. As with positive psychology, this secret is based on science, the scientific law of attraction (and if you doubt the scientific seriousness of this work, remember that Byrne mentions quantum physics). As with many others writing in this genre, Byrne has the appropriate sense of self-importance. She describes how she has discovered the 'secret' that other significant people had found before her. These forerunners include 'Plato, Shakespeare, Newton, Hugo, Beethoven, Lincoln, Emerson, Edison, Einstein.'[45] Hence we are in good company. And we, too, can find out the secret and become successful. As Byrne tells us, 'The secret can give you whatever you want.'[46]

The secret will bring happiness, good health and extraordinary wealth – and any other thing that you may wish for. So what is this secret? That thoughts are powerful and that you can use your thoughts to bring good things into existence. One way to think about this, metaphorically, is to imagine that we are like magnets. 'You are the most powerful magnet in the Universe! You contain a magnetic power within you that is more powerful than anything in this world, and this unfathomable magnetic power is emitted through your thoughts.'[47] As a magnet, you attract what you want, and engender success through the power of your mind.

This is difficult to treat with any seriousness. As Catherine Bennett writes in the *Guardian*, 'only an idiot can take The Secret seriously.'[48] All the same, there are people who seem to follow the advice. One person who she claims believes this is David Cameron. He concentrates on dreams and positive outcomes, not on depressing things. 'Observe how Secret practitioner Cameron only emphasizes the things he does want,' Bennett continues: 'Happiness, for example.'

And this is the most remarkable feat of *The Secret*: its ability to defend inequality. While the 99 per cent has become a worldwide slogan questioning the concentration of wealth, the author of *The Secret* offers an alternative view of the situation. 'Why do you think that 1 percent of the population earns around 96 percent of all the money that's being earned?', Bob Proctors is asked rhetorically in the book, answering, 'People who have drawn wealth into their lives used The Secret, whether consciously or unconsciously. They think thoughts of abundance and wealth, and they do not allow any contradictory thoughts to take root in their minds.'[49]

This vision is not just delusional; it is also cruel. What it says is that we bring our own destiny upon ourselves. As Ehrenreich puts it, '[T]he flip side of positivity is thus a harsh insistence on personal responsibility.'[50] This implies that all of the drawbacks that one might experience are not the product of a complex series of circumstances, but ultimately down to one's own doing. Losing one's job is not the result of economic circumstances; it is a product of one's own attitude. Surviving breast cancer is not simply about receiving professional treatment; it is about your will-power and whether you have put your mind to it. As Byrne claims: 'Illness cannot exist in a body that has harmonious thoughts.' What about natural catastrophes? Asked this question after the 2004 tsunami, Byrne explains: 'By the law of attraction, they [the victims] had to be on the same frequency as the event.'[51]

What makes Byrne so relevant to our analysis of bio-morality is that she expresses, in an extreme form, a sentiment which is prevailing not just in new-age circles, but also in politics. Byrne's insistence on the individual and his or her personal responsibility is the perfect corollary to a politics which aims to legitimize injustice, poverty and class division. Poor people are not structurally discriminated against; they simply lack sufficient thought power.

Meanwhile, we are comforted that widening gaps in society are not necessarily a bad thing since studies have revealed that those who are poor are just as likely to be happy as those who are better off. Exactly what is meant by happiness here remains unclear. As we will now see, it is not a particularly stable thing which we can easily capture.

Who Is Happy?

How do we know that we are happy? Can we ever find out? Academic accounts would say no. Indeed, if our circumstances make no difference – if I will be no more happy from winning a million dollar lottery than from losing both my arms in a car crash – then how, frankly, can we even begin to think about happiness as something you either have or do not have? How do we apply this scale?

While politicians and researchers tirelessly continue to dig for new concepts and measures of happiness (conveniently forgetting that St Augustine, around 400 CE, listed 289 different theoretical accounts of happiness[52]), we seem to avoid this question in everyday parlance. It is unlikely that you would hear the question, 'How happy are you today?'

A more acceptable question, which we tend to ask instead, is 'How's it going?' This seemingly innocent saying has attracted well-deserved suspicion. Pascal Bruckner subjects this phrase to detailed philosophical scrutiny. 'How's it going?' he says, 'is the most futile and the most profound of questions.'[53] On the one hand it does not really ask anything. It is irritatingly sweeping and extraordinarily imprecise, suggesting that you may want to offer a broad description of how things are going, such as how the weather might be and whether or not you got that job you recently applied for. You pile up a series of objective features, suggesting that somehow this relates to your general wellbeing. But on the other hand, this is a question that forces you into a corner. You are expected to offer a thoroughgoing moral account of yourself. Bruckner points out it is 'a way of intimating something: we want to force the person met to situate himself, we want to petrify him, subject him to a detailed examination'.[54] The not-so-innocent nature of this question is that it forces you to accumulate all the available information about yourself and your circumstances and to quickly assemble a coherent picture that would please the interrogator. The picture, of course, will have little to do with you. And whatever your interlocutor may think of the account – he or she might be very pleased, who knows? – you will nevertheless crumble beneath the weight of these words.

But what Bruckner, in his otherwise excellent analysis, fails to properly capture is the irreconcilable tension between the two subjects that are at play here. These are teased out in another fascinating analysis of this same saying. Alenka Zupančič writes the following about *how's it going*:

> The greatness of this formula resides in the fact that the usual answer (*Very well, thank you*) leaves wonderfully intact the ambiguity of this question, its two possible 'subjects.' In order to see this, it is enough to shift the accent a little and to emphasize the 'it' in 'How's it going.' What I have in mind is that the full answer to the question *How's it going?* might very well be something like: It is going very well. But me – well, that's another matter. I'm tired, I'm depressed, my back aches…[55]

Even to get the first thing right – to make the *it* go 'very well' – seems an ambitious and difficult feat. This is also the theme of one of Bourdieu's more fascinating books, where he follows a number of people, mainly couples from middle-class families, as they embark on what we may call project *it*. These projects involve finding the perfect house, in the right kind of suburb, with a garden for the kids to play in and a private parking spot where they can wash and polish their car. But, as Bourdieu remarks, these projects are often too large for them. They 'lock themselves into impossible constraints, with no option but to cope with the consequences of their decisions'.[56] So now they sit there, isolated, in their houses, far away from the city. They spend their days commuting, back and forth, to the office, driving through a thick traffic jam. They are condemned to yo-yo between schools and sports activities, collecting and dropping off children, both their own and others'. It's tempting to put oneself in this situation, as they drive into the garage, longing for that moment of vegetative silence in front of the TV they will soon enjoy, when the children have finally fallen asleep. These are the 'foundations of petit-bourgeois suffering', as Bourdieu calls them.

This is one side of the duty to be happy. You must try to make your life appear happy, whether by buying a house, getting married or taking on some other great life project. Lauren Berlant calls these projects 'good-life fantasies'.[57] They rest on traditional middle-class dreams that have become increasingly untenable – or unachievable – for today's bourgeoisie. They remain optimistic, but this cognitive stance is based on delusional assumptions about meritocracy and the possibility of upward social mobility.

Failing to please the *it* can be a painful experience. The debt accumulates; you are made redundant; and you can no longer pay your mortgage. When the whole *it*-thing is going to hell, you have to look for alternative projects – for what we may call 'project *you*'. What remains now, amid the depressing graveyard of good-life fantasies, is to shut out the external world and to concentrate more intensively on the self – *your* self. Sure, this inward turn is also employed by those who have moderately succeeded with their *it*-projects. The focus on yourself can be a pleasant experience, where the constant terror of life is momentarily put on pause. Meanwhile we listen to ourselves, the bodies we have, and elevate our pulsating corporeal murmurings to some form of truth, a *telos* of life.

This is an age-old tension between self-image and the prevailing norms and values of the day. Take ancient Greece. Or, to be more precise, take Aristotle and his vision of happiness, and what he, and others at the time, would call *eudaimonia*. This is the ancient Greek equivalent of happiness. Yet it has little in common with Deepak Chopra. For Aristotle, *eudaimonia* was not something you would accidentally stumble upon or bring into being by lying down on a beach listening to sentimental music. *Eudaimonia* is about the good life, and a version of happiness that is charged with political meaning. The good life, for the Greeks, was not an isolated matter, where an individual self would live separately from others. Neither was it primarily about sensory pleasures or what the body would whisper to us. Living well and acting well are the prerequisites for a happy life. It is through your virtuous actions that you create a good life.

But this was no mean feat. For Aristotle, a happy man had to dedicate himself, wholeheartedly, to a life of virtue, in keeping only with the highest human faculties. Such life, he claimed, had to be balanced: desires, for example, must not be expressed, unless in a tempered and moderate fashion; bravery and courage are absolutely necessary, but must not be so exhibited as to come out on the other side as bragging or self-indulgence.

There is something both ascetical and aristocratic at play here. You have to renounce your immediate inclinations and repress your desires. Those who fail to resist such temptations, and fall into a world of immediate pleasures, will remain at the level of 'grazing animals', as Aristotle contemptuously called these 'other' people. And what's more, to transform yourself into a person of great virtue you have to put in the hours. No cheating; no short-cuts. So don't put your faith in books like *Happiness Now*.

Happiness, according to Aristotle, is a harmonization between the virtuous actions taken by an individual and the values handed down to society by the gods. The good life is the life of the gods. So, follow the gods, reads the advice. Look at them, and learn. But whatever you do, don't ever believe you are on the same level. As in the hierarchical world of drug cartels, you need to respect boundaries, and tread lightly. Avoid hubris. Or expect your fate.

If Aristotle is the philosopher we might associate with 'project it', it is Jean-Jacques Rosseau that we would have to link to 'project I'.

Sure, this association is somewhat unfortunate. Rousseau could not have predicted the afterlife of his ideas; and one may suspect, had he known that many of his thoughts would be hi-jacked by the so-called 'self-help gurus', he would not have been overly pleased. As Terry Eagleton remarked in a recent essay, Rousseau, as a precursor to Marx, would be appalled by the 'drastic shrinking of the public sphere',[58] let alone the blind celebration of individual narcissism.

That aside, Rousseau's vision of happiness was distinctly separate from Aristotle. In *Reveries of a Solitary Walker*, he describes happiness as a peaceful resting-place,

> with no need to remember the past or reach in to the future, where time is nothing to it, where the present runs on indefinitely but this duration goes unnoticed, with no sign of the passing of time, and no other feeling of deprivation or enjoyment, pleasure or pain, desire or fear than the simple feeling of existence, a feeling that fills our soul entirely, as long as this state lasts, we can call ourselves happy....[59]

Unlike Aristotle, this vision of happiness pays no attention to virtues or actions. On the contrary, this is a description of happiness that completely ignores action. Rousseau sees happiness as a state of being, where the existence of the self is absorbed by the present. He describes lying on the bottom of a boat that drifts aimlessly on a lake.

Pleasant as this image may seem, it brings us to a classic philosophical problem of happiness, noted by Robert Nozick.[60] You will recall this from the film *The Matrix*. The problem is this. Imagine there is a machine that could produce any experience you most desire; imagine now that you let yourself be operated on by some experimental neuropsychologists who could stimulate your brain and give you the experience of doing all of those things that give your life sense and purpose (meeting friends, falling in love, reading a book, and so on). The only problem is that you don't do these things. You just float around in a tank and your body and brain are attached to electrodes. Would you plug into this machine? Or the question posed to Neo in *The Matrix*: would you take the blue pill, or the red pill?

What defines our present relationship to happiness is that we want to pursue both happiness projects. While happiness has become associated with a particular countenance – to express our true self, and to display our positive features – we can also observe the emergence of novel forms of escape fantasies that, in various ways, reproduce Rousseau's aimless boat trip, or disappearing into a massive tank, or swallowing the blue pill. To appreciate this desire, we need to consider the emergence of a new demand. It is not just the demand to be happy. It is the demand to enjoy every turn in your life, and to make every instance a potential moment for enjoyment. As we will see, this is where the superego will raise its ugly head again.

Too Much Happiness

The imperative to pursue happiness marks a peculiar shift. If society was traditionally founded on prohibition – in which you had to restrain yourself and suppress your desires in order to fit in (or avoid being killed) – we have now entered an era where we are not just allowed, but morally commanded, to express our desires. As Bruckner puts it, '[T]he requirement of the secular goal of happiness is that it must be realized without delay.'[61] Forget about the previous age of delayed gratification when it was only after working hours that you could express yourself, and allow yourself something extra. Now we can – and should – be happy, 24/7.

As our attempts to bring about happiness have become ever more extreme, the limitations have become painfully palpable, as with the story about Andrew Park, who thought it was a good idea to celebrate Christmas every day, with a decorated Christmas tree and new gifts waiting for him each morning. But the ceremony did not deliver the happiness it was meant to.[62] The compulsive insistence on the same did not morph into the discovery of the new. It was just that: the same. It became repetitive, monotonous, exhausting.

This mode of incessant repetition is the theme of Steve McQueen's film *Shame*. Michael Fassbender, playing the main character Brandon, remains mute throughout the film, with only a few exceptions. We see almost as much of his half-erected penis as his lips, and whenever the latter are moving, they say less than nothing. He has arranged his life according to the principle of maximum enjoyment. Masturbation. Sex. Cocaine. Meaningless work (with occasional breaks for more masturbation). And then back again to his overpriced, soulless condo. One scene in particular captures this sense of passive nihilism: after another pointless day at the office, Brandon comes home, puts on a recording of Bach's Goldberg Variations, takes out a bottle of beer and a box of leftover Asian food, sits down in his kitchen, pops open his laptop and puts on some hard-core porn. No doubt, a meal worthy of the man of now.

On the surface, *Shame* describes a middle-aged sex addict who has become trapped in a self-destructive pattern of behaviour. He is depressed, but not depressed in the classical sense. We might think that his problem is that he is incapable of gaining pleasure. But it is the other way round; he is incapable of doing anything else apart from pursuing pleasure.

This is a state that Mark Fisher has described as depressive hedonia.[63] It is not the anhedonia that we normally associate with depression, but a depression that comes out of relentless hedonism. It is a state in which nothing exists apart from the repetitive pursuit of pleasure, where one is perfectly aware that something fundamental is missing, yet incapable of looking anywhere beyond the constant rush after indulgence. This produces a claustrophobic sense of boredom.

Steve McQueen explained in an interview that he was interested in making a film about 'now', and how the availability of something, in this case sex, will inevitably make us over-consume, endlessly, like a bunch of unruly children unleashed on a table piled with candy. 'It's like there's more fatty food in supermarkets, so people get fat.'[64] But the film resists the temptation to moralize. Brandon is not a simple victim of consumer society, who has been lured into glamorizing the superficial, at the expense of the real thing. The problem that Brandon experiences is the opposite: he gets too much of the real thing.

We know from psychoanalysis that pleasure and excessive enjoyment (or *jouissance*) are two dramatically different things. While the pleasure principle prescribes small and regulated doses of pleasure in order to restrain pain and suffering, excessive enjoyment disregards any such calculations. It would be easy to say that Brandon opts for the latter, that his entire being is geared towards excess. But that would be to miss the point. What makes Brandon interesting for our analysis of biomorality is that, in spite of never finding the object of his desire, he unwillingly continues to search for more pleasures to consume. These are not necessarily grandiose pleasures, but an endless series of mundane activities – all of which are assumed, somewhat naïvely, to bring purpose to his life. As such, he is strangely loyal to the wellness command: he does not drive recklessly towards excess and death, but pursues pleasures. Yet, death and excess are his inexorable destination.

This paradox helps us explain the ambiguity of the wellness command. We mentioned at the beginning of this book that the wellness command has much in common with what Žižek calls the superego injunction to enjoy. In both instances we are pushed to pursue something that seems to produce its opposite. The more we seek to enjoy, the more difficult it becomes. The more we try to maximize our wellness, the more we seem to suffer. But to come to terms with this ambiguity it is crucial to ask what enjoyment means. Or more specifically: what kind of enjoyment is implied in that injunction? Are we dealing with moderate pleasures, or excessive enjoyment? In *The Parallax View*, Žižek remarks: '[A]re not injunctions to have a good time, to acquire self-realization and self-fulfillment, and so on, precisely injunctions to *avoid* excessive *jouissance*, to find a kind of homeostatic balance?'[65]

This would definitely be the case with the wellness command: it is designed to help maintain a sense of balanced wellbeing, whether that involves taking up a healthy eating habit, exercising more or improving our mindfulness skills. What all these activities have in common is a commitment to homeostasis and balance, to produce a functioning non-excessive person.

Yet this is only part of the story. Žižek continues: '[T]he commodified provocations to enjoy which bombard us all the time push us toward, precisely, an autistic-masturbatory, "asocial" *jouissance* whose supreme case is drug addiction.'[66]

And this is the ambiguity at the heart of the wellness syndrome. On the one hand, we are bombarded with the command at all times and places to seek pleasure, a moderate form of pleasure, which is devoid of excessive enjoyment. This form of lifestyle, dictated by the rules of the pleasure principle, we think will help to maintain a pleasant, balanced life. This is all fine, it seems. But then the constant pressure to seek pleasure becomes boring and exhausting. It pushes us to what Žižek calls an autistic-masturbatory, 'asocial' *jouissance*. At this point, the pursuit of pleasure has brought about an isolated existence defined by the brutal meaninglessness of the body. This is the case with Brandon. In his commitment to bodily pleasure, he has become trapped in a repetitive loop of desire. Every encounter with a desired object leaves him cold, and ultimately depressed. He moves from object to object, metonymically, receiving nothing by way of satisfaction. He sits there, at his kitchen table, indolently watching porn. That is where the command to enjoy has taken him, to its logical conclusion: an encounter with the emptiness of his own desire.

The great tragedy of Brandon is that he has mistaken his body for a truth system. While his world continues to disappoint, he puts more and more faith in his own body for consolation. This is the fate of the passive nihilist. Detached, he looks at the world and finds it meaningless. For him, truth does not exist out there. It lies within, deep inside the amazing mysteries of the self. As such, he subscribes to the ideals of biomorality.

At this point, proponents of wellness are likely to protest. For them, Brandon is about as far from the perfect biomoral life as you can get. He is a porn-obsessed, alienated office worker in acute need of meditation, mindfulness and a more healthy diet. If only he could develop a more positive outlook on life and work towards authentic happiness, he would realize that milder forms of pleasures, like a quiet walk in the park, are far more satisfying than an endless loop of hardcore porn.

Yet Brandon is closer to the happiness-seeker than we might think. While preferring porn to yoga, he relies on no other messages or signals than those emitted from his body. Brandon, like any good wellness-seeker, pursues satisfaction in a calculated and repetitive manner, seeking out what he believes to be a safe source of pleasure. The life of both Brandon and other wellness-seekers becomes almost completely oriented around maximizing their own happiness. As this obsession slowly edges out the rest of the world, what is left is the repetitive pulsation of the body.

4

The Chosen Life

Plato says that the unexamined life is not worth living. But
what if the examined life turns out to be a clunker as well?

Kurt Vonnegut, *Wampeters, Foma and
Granfalloons*, 1974[1]

The Promise of Unemployment

To unleash our untapped human potential we are required
to embark on a long journey inwards. Every conceivable
aspect, from our inner emotions to our daily habits, needs
to be examined and subsequently corrected and optimized.
This requires a determinate orientation and a relentlessly
positive attitude. Even when our situation appears infinitely
grim, we are requested to remain optimistic, search inside
of ourselves and come up with a solution. As such, positivity
is the pathway to success. It is the key to finding a partner
you love and friends you can spend time with. But more than
that, it is the key to finding a job and a flourishing career.
Nowhere is the message of positivity more loudly rehearsed
than in job seeking. 'You've followed every bit of career
advice but still no luck with your job hunt?' the career coach
Harry Freedman rhetorically asks. 'The answer could be
positive thinking.'[2]

The 52-year-old John Robson from Wigan, UK, did not feel particularly positive the day his jobseekers' allowance was cut. He had been sanctioned, which means that he would now have to apply for hardship payments. He was down to about half of the jobseeker's allowance, or £30 a week. Robson had not been notified in advance. He only found out when the money did not appear in his account. The Jobcentre accused him of having missed the deadline for three jobs, although he had indeed applied. The applications had just arrived late.

In April 2011, a Jobcentre Plus adviser blew the whistle. He told the *Guardian* that they systematically tricked jobseekers into losing their benefits.[3] Dyslexics were given written job searches they found difficult to deal with. Application forms were deliberately sent out at the last minute, so that jobseekers would not manage to send off their application in time. These were not private initiatives, orchestrated by some ill-spirited Jobcentre workers. The directive had come from above. The advisers had simply followed the dictates given to them. In fact, the adviser that the *Guardian* talked to described how he and his colleagues had been accused of lagging behind other offices, which had proved much more efficient in getting people sanctioned. As one Jobcentre adviser put it, '[W]e were far behind other offices, and we went to a meeting where they compared us with other offices, and said we now have to do three a week to catch up. Most staff go into work and they're thinking about it from moment one – who am I going to stop this week?'[4]

The UK Department of Work and Pensions (DWP) initially denied that Jobcentres were deliberately tricking vulnerable people into losing their welfare entitlements. After the news broke, the Work and Pensions Secretary, Iain Duncan Smith, appeared on Sky News, where he called the story 'a conspiracy'.[5] But the DWP later admitted that some Jobcentres had been applying targets, although these were claimed to be isolated incidents.

This 'bad apple' theory was contested in 2013, when a newsletter from the Malvern Jobcentre was leaked. In the letter it was stated that the Jobcentre workers had been too slow in sanctioning their claimants. From the letter: '[W]e are currently one of the worst performing offices with sanction benefit referrals and unless we improve we will be put under special measures.'[6] It was later revealed that the DWP produced national sanctions 'scorecards', where the performance is broken down by district, with red and green arrows suggesting whether the district is performing well or not.[7] The more people you sanction, the better your performance. As one adviser puts it: 'Saving the public purse is the catchphrase that is used in our office.'[8]

The official reason for sanctioning jobseekers is that they have been inactive in their search. They haven't applied for enough jobs, they have missed deadlines, or they have failed to appear for training activities designed to improve their employability. In short, they have failed to live up to the expectations involved in job seeking.

In a strange way, being sanctioned is rather like being fired from a job, on the grounds that you have shirked your duties. Yet this analogy is not so strange, since jobseeking is now regarded as a job itself. In his one-year study of an American support organization for unemployed West Coasters, the organizational theorist Ofer Sharone observed that the unemployed were seen as professional workers. Job seeking was seen as a serious occupation; not just something you did on the side. 'View your search as a full time job, not a part time job,'[9] one of the experts at the support group told the jobseekers.

But what kind of job is job seeking? It is not simply an administrative job, which involves sending off numerous applications and fine-tuning your CV. It is more about sales and product development. Sales in the sense that you need to come up with new ways to market, brand and sell yourself. Product development in the sense that you need to find new ways to refine, enhance and change yourself. After all, as a jobseeker you have to see yourself as a product, one which has to be made attractive on the market. The catch-phrase is to make yourself employable – attractive enough for an employer to take you on board. Important here is to package yourself as a healthy, upbeat and positive talent in waiting.

Over the course of the latter part of the twentieth century, employability took on a distinct meaning. Initially it was introduced to separate those who could work from those who couldn't, and then devise political initiatives that could help the borderline cases to get into employment. In other words, it was a political initiative where the emphasis was placed on what employers could do to attract workers to enter the labour market.[10]

While this demand-led model underwent a series of revisions during the 1960s and 1970s, it was largely in place until the early 1990s. At about this time, a novel approach to employability was beginning to take shape. This came to be known as 'labour market performance employability'.[11] At this juncture, although the focus was shifting towards the individual, it was still acknowledged that employment was not entirely an individual affair.

It is not until the late 1990s that we get the present-day version of employability, where the individual stands alone as the responsible agent, as someone who is assumed to be fully flexible, constantly malleable and exceedingly adaptable. This is a shift towards what some have called supply-led fundamentalism.[12] The birth of this fundamentalism can be traced back to 1998 in the United Kingdom, when Tony Blair introduced the New Deal; and 1996 in the United States, when Bill Clinton signed a new welfare reform bill. They had both attacked the welfare system for being helplessly ineffective. And the most serious problem, they claimed, was that the welfare state had become conducive to passivity and laziness. The system was producing people who would automatically drift into a phlegmatic state, where they were assumed to feed off the generous welfare system. This was the birth of the Welfare Queen in the United States, and her British cousin, the chavette. As described in Chapter 2, this involved a pejorative image of a single mother with multiple children, who collected money from the state. They were assumed to have unhealthy lifestyles, anti-social tendencies and a negative attitude to work. The new welfare reforms of the mid-1990s were targeted precisely at these morally defiled individuals. Now they would have to develop an upbeat, 'can-do' attitude.

As he signed the legislation, Clinton made good on his 1992 election promise 'to end welfare as we know it'.[13] In many ways, he would institute the politics that was initially conceived by Reagan, who cleverly combined his attack on the welfare state with a deliberate strategy to charm the emerging generation of self-actualizers. In the United Kingdom, the story was similar. When Blair took office in 1997, he was devising a series of initiatives that helped bureaucratize Thatcherite politics while appealing to the authenticity-seeking middle classes. Indeed, Blair's blunt turn to the right did not pass unnoticed. While many people would see this as a regrettable move in the wrong direction, others were delighted. One of them was Margaret Thatcher. In 2002, when she was invited to a dinner in Hampshire, one of the guests asked what was her greatest achievement. Her response: 'Tony Blair and New Labour'.[14]

Here is the irony. What came out of this distinct political turn – a new notion of employability, resting on a harsh insistence on individual responsibility – was soon regarded as non-political. This is much the same observation that Sharone makes in his study of American jobseekers: that employability has become radically depoliticized. Whatever the structural dimension may be to unemployment, these issues are best left unmentioned. The jobseekers whom Sharone met in the support group were encouraged not to look for external obstacles, such as the bleak labour market. They were told to direct their gaze inwards: to penetrate, examine and finally overcome the internal obstacles. To improve their chances of succeeding, they were told to spend all of their time with those who would keep them positive. The jobseekers were also asked to block out other unpleasant aspects, which they could do by avoiding the news (going on a 'news fast', as they called it). Negative words should also be avoided, especially the word 'unemployed', which they had banned altogether. 'You are not unemployed,' one of the experts told the jobseekers, 'you are free agents.'[15]

This kind of language displaces structural issues onto the individual. If you can't get a job, it is not due to the economy or any other external causes. It is because of *your* inability to overcome your inner obstacles. Or it is because you insist on looking in the wrong places, as we are told in the self-help manual *Unlock the Hidden Job Market*, by Duncan Mathison and Martha I. Finney. Their claim is that there are two types of job markets. First there is the market that everyone knows about. And listen, that's not where you will find a job! There are too many people fighting there already. Look carefully and you will discover that there is another market, too – the hidden job market, 'that secret parallel universe of opportunities that are waiting for anyone with the skill, curiosity, and energy to seek them out'.[16] This, the authors go on to tell us, is where you will find your jobs. You just need to proactively impose yourself into this hidden sphere. You need to take an active role in your job search, and don't let your courteous manner stand in the way. 'It's not rude to intrude,'[17] as they put it.

What we get here is a twist on the Swedish saying: 'There is no bad weather, just bad clothes.' Applied to job seeking it becomes: 'There are no bad economic times, just bad jobseekers.'

The jobseekers Sharone talked to seemed to have fully adopted ideas of self-help and individual responsibility. At first, these ideas gave them a momentary sense of autonomy and agency. They even gave them a sense of excitement. But these positive feelings were later replaced by a sense of dejection and self-blame. For some, this would come after six weeks. For others, it took up to three months. What they all had in common, though, was that at no time would they 'resist the ideological claim that finding a job is within their control'.[18] Indeed, never did they mention the labour market and the fact that few jobs seemed to be out there. Instead they internalized their defeat, placing the responsibility on themselves, which, of course, resulted in intense self-hatred. As one of the members put it: 'The *hardest* thing is feeling that there is something wrong with me that I am not finding a job.' Or another: 'I feel like a loser.'[19]

If the unemployed come to be seen as professional workers, then an increasingly large proportion of workers have become constructed as soon-to-be unemployed. This is the dark side of the new spirit of capitalism. It is well known that labour relations have become more flexible over the last three decades, mainly as a result of globalization, deregulation and economic liberalization. The relatively stable standard employment associated with the Fordist era, where employees could expect to work with the same employer throughout their lives, is now a distant memory. For the generation coming of age in the late 1960s this was a relief. Stable employment had become synonymous with conventional institutions, and these institutions were widely despised because they were thought to suppress, and even suffocate, the soul. For this generation, the idea of working in the same place all their lives was out of the question. With the gradual disappearance of these life-regulating agencies, a new reality began to emerge, one in which the individual was constructed as a free agent. As Andrew Ross writes in *Nice Work If You Can Get It*: 'In return for giving up the tedium of stable employment in a large hierarchical organization, would-be free agents are buzzed by the thrill of proving themselves by finding out if they have what it takes to prevail in the heady swim of self-employment.'[20] What the liberation from these institutions offers by way of new-won freedom, however, is taken away in terms of security. As a result, it becomes difficult to look ahead, plan and dream of a future.

Existence is divided into smaller units, with a timeline that is constantly shrinking. Without the possibility of going back in time, these people find themselves in a game where the dream of winning has been replaced by the hope of survival. It is about making it to the next round, when it's your time to throw the dice again, hoping that luck will come your way. Andrew Ross again: 'Once they are in this game, some of the players thrive, but most subsist, neither as employers nor traditional employees, in a limbo of uncertainty, juggling their options, massaging their contacts, managing their over-committed time, and developing coping strategies for handling the uncertainty of never knowing where their next project, or source of income, is coming from.'[21]

What is new here is not the insecurity as such. People have always been pushed to the margins, thrown into an uncertain position, where they don't know whether they will be able to earn money through their own work. What is new is that this uncertainty is combined with an ethos of self-actualization, self-development, self-growth and self-help. As a free agent you are forced to make yourself visible, express yourself and attract the attention of interested employers. However destitute you may be, you have to present yourself as a possible winner, as someone who is positive and forward-looking.

It is hard to construct an energetic and positive persona when the actual experience is more akin to depression. To overcome such obstacles, jobseekers are asked to put on a convincing performance. The jobseekers whom Ofer Sharone followed were asked to develop a thirty-second commercial of themselves that had to be performed in a smooth and convincing manner. They were even asked to imagine they were delivering their own personal commercial to Bill Gates as they rode in an elevator to the twentieth floor.

The need to put on a performance can also be found in Ivor Southwood's insider account of unemployment. Among the endless stream of emails from various job agencies, he received one with the subject header: 'Britain's got talent.

What's yours, Ivor?'[22] The patronizing tone (insinuating that the recipient doesn't really have any notable talents) is unmistakable. But there is something else in that subject header that calls for attention, and that is how jobseeking now seems to have become its own talent show.

'The traditional way of applying for jobs seems to be on the way out,' Lucy Tobin writes in the *Guardian*.[23] 'The new way to recruit', she continues, 'is to think like Simon Cowell, or do a Lord Sugar: turn a job interview into a reality TV-style set of tasks, ask for poems, songs, presentations or videos; and even encourage voting for the "winner."' The trend is that jobseekers are asked to add something extra and unexpected to their presentations, like the young man described in the article, who had prepared a choreographed PowerPoint so the images appeared when he moved his hands.

Human resource departments of companies seem to have taken this message to heart. In September 2011, a luxury hotel in Sweden arranged a large-scale job audition for prospective cleaners – 1,800 young people showed up. Many of them were living far away from the venue, and had been transported by bus. While waiting in the queue they were interviewed by a TV team. At the stage, they were given two minutes to impress the jury.[24] The same technique was used when recruiting waiters and dishwashers for the Stockholm themepark Gröna Lund. Here, the interviewees were called 'artists'. Before entering the stage they had to wait 'backstage' (the employee locker room). And to enter the premises they needed a 'backstage pass' (swipe card).

Underpinning these show-business techniques is the wider notion of talent. Many management gurus offer executives advice in winning the 'war for talent'. The core of talent management is to recruit top performers, reward them disproportionately and rapidly push them into senior positions. This is now a relatively established management doctrine, which has survived long enough to escape the fad label. The reason why it has maintained its popularity over time, and now has become part of mainstream human resource management, is not that it works particularly well. In fact, it often results in under-experienced people having vast responsibilities with which they cannot cope. Talent management is popular because it helps legitimize and normalize horrendously inflated pay cheques. 'This "talent mind-set" is the new orthodoxy of American management,' Malcolm Gladwell wrote more than a decade ago. 'It is the intellectual justification for why such a high premium is placed on degrees from first-tier business schools, and why the compensation packages for top executives have become so lavish.'[25] According to this line of thought, it is entirely acceptable that some people are rewarded inordinately while others are left empty handed. This, of course, is the alluring principle of the talent shows, too. Every now and then, someone appears on stage, someone who has found within him- or herself a hidden talent, a talent that will open up new possibilities, new adventures and a new way of life.

That this mindset is spreading from corporations to other spheres of working life is perhaps worrying. Clearly not everyone can, or indeed should, be an exceptional 'talent'. By putting such a strong emphasis on talent is to remind the 'untalented' majority that they are worthless. What is more, the state seems to be a willing participant in the process. The buses that were hired to take the aspiring artists to the audition – the one that offered a job in the luxury hotel – were paid for by the state. The event was jointly organized by Arbetsförmedlingen, the Swedish equivalent of the British Jobcentres.

These shows remind us that technical skills are not enough (in some cases, significant experience and good qualifications could be a negative). What is really demanded is a particular self, one that is positive, healthy and energetic. While turning to others for support and advice – and as we know, there is a whole army of life coaches, employment advisers and personal branding experts on hand to help us – we receive the same message: that we need to take responsibility for ourselves. We must nurture, track and package

our talent in a way that others will find appealing. As we
will now see, some have gone to great lengths to do so.

Know Yourself, Control Yourself, Improve yourself

In 2009, Chris Dancy was laid off. The prospects of finding
a new job were bleak. 'I didn't think I had a chance of being
employable,' he said in an interview with *Wired Magazine*.[26]
But Dancy was determined to do what he could to 'rebuild
himself for the future'. His strategy to become attractive on
the job market again was to build on a longstanding passion
of his. 'I've always liked measuring myself,' he says. The
transition from having his height monitored while growing
up, and his finances 'religiously tracked' in his twenties, to
the emerging culture of self-tracking seemed natural. For
him, there is not a single instance of life that should not be
measured. Indeed, if something *could* be measured, then it
also *should* be measured. 'If you can measure it, someone
will, and that somebody should be you,' as he puts it. And
indeed, there are many things that can now be transformed
into data, for us (or for others) to analyse. For Dancy, the
philosophy is simple: the more you can find out, the better.
He is connected to at least three sensors. 'Sometimes, it's as
much as five. They measure his pulse, his REM sleep, his
skin temperature, and more. He also has sensors all over his
house. There's even one on his toilet so he can look for cor-
relations between his bathroom habits and his sleep patterns.'[27] This is the examined life to which the wo/man of
now is sentenced. It is not the philosophical examination
described by Socrates (in Plato's *Apology*), through which
one could confront life in a more honest manner. (Socrates
uttered these words after choosing death rather than exile.)
But examination for the self-tracker is not about confronting
existential questions or accepting the limitations of human
life. It is about making oneself better adapted to the conditions of the market. As such, the examined life, as Vonnegut
reminds us, can be a clunker as well.

Dancy is no longer unemployed. It was his online presence, he explains, that helped him find a new job. He has no plans to stop his exercises in self-tracking. They turned out to be productive, by making him employable, but also helping him stay competitive. These days, it is not just for personal benefit that Dancy engages in this extreme form of self-examination. The same method is applied to his work, where he is now recording and storing everything that he does in his professional life. In other words, he is more productive both as an individual and as an employee, although, to him, the difference between the two is merely incidental.

Recording and presenting one's life, like Dancy does, is now common practice among members of the rapidly growing 'quantified self movement'. With the gym junkie's desire to perfect his or her work-out, and the nerd's hope to transcend the world with superior smarts, this movement has given a new significance to numbers. According to one of the movement's founders, Gary Wolf, self-quantification promises 'self knowledge through numbers'.[28] The goal is simply to improve oneself. But where the philosophical idea of improvement remains ambiguous, the method is straightforward: to capture in excruciating detail even the most minor aspects of life. And this is realized through the rise of relatively cheap 'wearable technologies' that incorporate sensors to capture data from our bodies. It began with the pedometer and heart rate monitor, followed by more advanced devices that record sleep patterns, skin responses, bodily movement and moods as well as surrounding environmental factors such as air quality. Users can then upload the data onto their computer and social media sites, where they are analysed and examined. They can look for co-variations in their heart rate and sleep, track the effect certain food has on their mood and figure out which locations make their brains more active. The final step is to compare their personal data with other self-quantifiers to identify common patterns. At so-called 'Show-and-Tells', self-trackers come to give short presentations about new forms of self-monitoring they have invented. Incidentally the audience finds out details such as when the presenter eats, sleeps, exercises and defecates.

In a recent report from *The Economist*, we meet an investment banker who used the technology to overcome sleep deprivation so he could become 'more relaxed, sharper and more switched on'.[29] Another self-quantifier did not just track himself, but had extended the technique to the rest of the family, recording, among other things, his wife's menstrual cycle.[30] A third enthusiast had developed an app which continuously inquired about her mood. She found that eating cup cakes on the way to work would put her in a bad mood later in the day.

How can we explain this compulsive drive towards recording oneself? It is not simply about getting rid of bad habits, such as excessive alcohol consumption or lack of exercise. For many self-quantifiers, the project goes much deeper. They use data to structure almost every aspect of their lives, whether personal or professional, in an attempt to become more productive. It is not so much about amending various flaws as reconfiguring the entire self, reforming it into a streamlined business.

One entrepreneur, interviewed by the *Financial Times*, described his life-logging as akin to 'running a start-up', saying that, 'I'm always looking at the numbers, always tracking how the business is going...that's under-the-hood information that you can only garner from analysing different data points. So I started doing that with myself.'[31]

Tracking yourself as if you were a business fits perfectly into the life of what Philip Mirowski has called 'the ideal neo-liberal agent'.[32] This person would be unlikely to know that she is neoliberal, because, to her, politics is less interesting than reconfiguring her body and enhancing her self. She is a self-proclaimed pragmatist who has understood the inexorable conditions of our time, one in which the self has to be examined, enhanced and expressed. She has come to 'the realization that she is not just an employee or student, but also simultaneously a product to be sold, a walking advertisement, a manager of her résumé, a biographer of her rationales, and an entrepreneur of her possibilities'.[33] For the neoliberal agent the body is no longer personal. It is not even political. Instead it is an enterprise which, to create maximum returns, needs careful monitoring and optimization.

Many members of the life-logging movement have taken this message to heart. The 'bio-hacker' David Asprey claims that life-logging will add many years to your life and improve your IQ, thus giving you a competitive advantage.[34] A similar line of argument is made by Tim Ferriss, author of the bestseller *4 Hour Work Week*. In his sequel, *The 4 Hour Body*, he offers a set of 'life hacking' techniques that promise increased mental clarity and physical fitness. The successful life-hacker, he maintains, will be able to perform on two hours' sleep, and can develop techniques to sustain an orgasm for up to fifteen minutes.[35]

While the promises of life-logging vary, the underlying message remains largely intact: that careful bodily monitoring will result in increased performance. It is a method to render yourself more productive.

The question that is left unanswered here is what we should do when we have become more productive. How should we use the time that has now been freed up? The answer, it seems, is to find new ways to be even more productive. The paradox, as Steven Poole writes in *The New Statesman*, 'is that it is all too easy to spend one's time researching how to acquire the perfect set of productivity tools and strategies without ever actually settling down to do something'. Poole continues, '[T]he obsessive dream of productivity becomes a perfectly effective defence against its own realisation.'[36] And all of the time that you save 'will surely add up, earning you hours more freedom to hunt and hoard ever more productivity tips, until you are a purely theoretical master at doing nothing of value in the most efficient way imaginable'.[37] Or, as Evgeny Morozov writes in his scathing critique of the quantified self movement: 'Average time saved by finding your car keys through lifelogging: five minutes. Average time lost to the tyranny of unnecessary niceties entailed by lifelogging: a lifetime.'[38]

While life-logging might be seen as a rather nerdy hobby by some, others have taken it more seriously. The hedge fund GLG Partners, for instance, has recently introduced software that tracks lifestyle factors such as sleep and diet and then correlates these against the performance of a group of traders. If any problems are flagged by this analysis, traders are offered coaching to help change their bodily routines. For the manager who instigated these life-logging techniques, there was nothing strange about this. He claimed that: 'Sportsmen and women have used these techniques for years to give themselves a competitive advantage and it makes sense to do it in the office as well.'[39]

It is not just the finance industry that has found these technologies useful. This practice of recording and managing employee's bodily habits is now spilling into other occupations. Reluctantly, the Chicago Teachers Union accepted a contract that required its members to become part of the Chicago Healthy Lives wellness programme. As part of the programme, teachers had to share biometric information (such as cholesterol, blood pressure, weight and body mass index), fill in a wellness assessment questionnaire (with questions about happiness, stress and other broader issues), check in and post information to websites, and engage in at least fifteen minutes of wellness-related activities a month. For those requiring extra support, wellness coaching was offered. Refusing was only an option to those willing to pay the penalty of $600.

With the emergence of new devices, employers have gained an unprecedented opportunity to track their employees. They can now monitor much more than just job-related performance. They can track and analyse something as fundamental as an employee's 'wellness' indicators. This opens up the employee's entire life to monitoring, reflection and manipulation. The move beyond measures of traditional performance – such as production of output or hours spent in the workplace – represents a stealthy reconfiguration of control. Now, even the most intimate activities are visible to the corporate gaze, including what we eat, how much we sleep and the amount we drink.

This seems to introduce a neo-Orwellian phase of complete control, which is vividly captured in Gilles Deleuze's 'Postscript on the Societies of Control'.[40] In this short text Deleuze argues that the site of control is no longer a disciplinary institution we enter into and then leave again. Schools or prisons may have been horrible experiences for those trapped there, but at least they had clear boundaries, and a discernible outside. In a society of control, Deleuze argues, these boundaries are not acknowledged. People are held prisoner in their own homes, schools extend their reach everywhere, and, of course, the workplace lurks in our pocket (via a ceaselessly buzzing smartphone). Control becomes a gas, shrouding and penetrating every pore of our life. This control is both beguiling and insidious.

For many enthusiasts, life-logging is not an imposition. Rather, it speaks to their desire for personal liberation. 'As a self-quantifier,' the dedicated adherent Mark Moschel describes, 'I see the potential to control my own health and to modify my behaviors to optimize the length and quality of my life.'[41] Statements such as these may appear bizarrely self-obsessed, especially if one emphasizes the *I* and the *my*. But one should also note the other words that are being used here: control, modify and optimize. If we emphasize these words, we seem to be encountering a more familiar language, one which is reminiscent of Fredrick Winslow Taylor's Scientific Management. As Nikil Saval claims, the rise of self-quantification and life-hacking has revived 'Taylor's dream of pure efficiency'.[42] This time, however, the stopwatch is not confined to the factory floor, but keeps ticking at all moments of life, even during our sleep. When we are 'liberated from threats or coercion', Saval continues, 'we scientifically manage ourselves'.

Saval reminds us that we should be careful not to dismiss the self-quantifiers' behaviour as an expression of their narcissism. It could be the other way round: that they have given up on their personal project, and have willingly handed over their bodies to the larger cause of productivity. This seems to have been the case with Chris Dancy, who at a relatively advanced age turned to self-tracking to make himself more employable. Sure, he liked measuring himself. But he was also doing this out of necessity. He is just doing now what everyone else will have to do in the near future: 'Dancy doesn't think that all tracking is necessarily positive, but he's fatalistic about the future. Even if workers reject more Orwellian surveillance from employers – or companies determine these measures to be counter-productive – individual workers will likely use self-tracking to gain a competitive advantage.'[43]

Life-hacking is not just the fatalistic realization that we are products to be sold on the market. The implicit message is much worse: we are products which, unless continuously upgraded, will rapidly become obsolete. Neoliberal agents may be depoliticized, but not because they are trapped in narcissistic dreams of future fame. Rather, they are trapped by the harsh realization that self-management is the only avenue available. This is also the point Jonathan Crary sets out in *24/7*. 'In actuality there is an imposed and inescapable uniformity to our compulsory labor of self-management,' he writes. 'The illusion of choice and autonomy is one of the foundations of this global system of auto-regulation.'[44]

Game Over

Perhaps the most remarkable feature of the neoliberal agent is his or her ability to reconcile self-actualization with conformity. For the self-quantifier, meticulously collecting data is not just about personal satisfaction; it is also about advancing one's productivity and competitiveness. To maintain an edge, one has to adapt to the prevailing rules and play the game.

Playing the game is no longer just a metaphor. Games have become a visible component of everyday life, with middle-aged men playing video games on the subway. But there is now a growing genre of games where the purpose is not so much to have fun or momentarily drift into a fantasy world. These games are designed to make people more effective and productive, whether as workers, parents, gym-goers or lovers. The purpose of these games is not to give the player a momentary break or an escape from reality. Rather, it is to help people adapt themselves to the harsh reality of life and its overwhelming expectations, whether those are to do with building a perfect body, a clean and orderly home or just improving your daily smile-rate. Attempts to reform personal behaviour are often regarded as boring, laborious and even disciplinary. With games, this is no longer the case. Like Mary Poppins, they make boring activities fun. 'A spoonful of sugar helps the medicine go down,' she sings while cheerfully dancing around tidying with the use of her magical thought-power (making clothes fly through the air, landing softly in the wardrobe). The technique works, and the wide-eyed children are soon cleaning their room. This is the idea of gamification: to apply the logic of games to real-world situations, making boring stuff fun.

But what, exactly, is the logic of these games? Apart from a more entertaining package, they are based on the same thing that children desire; the same thing that they get from their parents when they have done something good; indeed, what they get from the dentist when they have obediently sustained an open mouth in the clinic. Rewards! Games introduce rewards – badges, points or even money – which are then used as incentives, not just to make one continue playing the game, but to make one play more and better, so that you want to make it to the next level.

Gamification has become widely popular among corporations that want to develop more intimate ties to their customers. Starbucks, for instance, have designed an app that rewards their customers with badges and free drinks when they virtually check in to one of their coffee shops. Google News rewarded their more frequent readers with badges. Google explained that turning news reading into a game would make it more fun and motivate people to read more.

A similar logic has been applied to everyday problems such as managing personal relationships. Using the app Kahnoodle, you can turn your marriage into a game. Here is one user explaining how it works: 'If you do little things for your partner... you get signals your love tank is full. And if you don't, you'll get signals that your love tank is almost empty.'[45] A full love tank can then be used to assign rewards such as a comforting massage or kinky sex. The hope harboured by the users seems to be that by carefully monitoring their love tank, and receiving rewards, they can improve their relationship.

If you wish, it is now possible to gamify your entire life. Using an app called 'Epic Win', you can 'level up your life'. This application turns your personal to-do list into a game. You create an 'avatar' which then goes on a 'quest' by completing basic everyday tasks such as doing the laundry or answering emails. When these are completed, your avatar gets rewards which can be used to 'level up' and get 'epic loot' (such as new equipment for one's avatar). When using this app, 'you'll benefit from a tidy home, a more organised working day or succeeding in whatever life goals you wish to achieve,' the developer told the *Guardian*.[46]

This is also how gamification is justified: it uses the psychology of rewards to produce a desirable outcome. What is not to like about people improving their relationships or reading more news? Would this not make citizens happier, more enlightened and better equipped to cope with our world? And applied to dieting: who would not be better off losing some extra weight, especially if it could be made easy and painless, by nudging the person with suitable rewards.

Using rewards to shape people's behaviour was the core idea behind the behavioural psychology of B.F. Skinner. Experimenting with animals in controlled situations, Skinner found that organisms respond to rewards, and that those behaviours that are continuously rewarded become reinforced over time. Over the years, these ideas have been widely criticized. In academic circles, Noam Chomsky famously attacked Skinner in a series of publications, making the case that his assumption about the human mind as a clean slate was 'totally absurd, based on nothing'.[47] Beyond academia, behaviourism found its most damning critique in Stanley Kubrick's 1971 film *A Clockwork Orange*, based on the novel by Anthony Burgess.

It may appear surprising that Skinner's work has made such a successful comeback, especially in an age of individual choice and self-actualization. Nothing should appear more offensive to the wo/men of now than submitting themselves to authoritarian commands. Even so, the Skinnerian idea of behavioural modification rests on the assumption that willpower is hugely limited. Interviewed in *The Atlantic* about weight-loss programmes, the behavioural scientist Jean Harvey-Berino said, 'Willpower doesn't work. What works heavily relies on Skinner – shaping behavior over time by giving feedback, and setting up environments where people aren't stimulated to eat the wrong foods.'[48]

Here, again, we are confronted with the paradoxical relationship between authority and conformity, on the one hand, and individual expression and self-actualization, on the other. Surrendering to an authoritarian agency, which is not just telling you what to do, but also handing out rewards and punishments to shape your behaviour more effectively, seems like undermining your own agency and autonomy.

But the perception has changed. As the self-trackers of the quantified self movement have adopted the techniques, Skinnerian behaviourism has become fashionable again. Rather than being a contradiction to the libertarian ideals of the life-loggers, Skinner is an extension, allowing them to concentrate on self-enhancement. But these methods have gone beyond the innovators and early adopters, and are now widely available to the masses. Anyone can download Skinnerian apps to their phones or computers. One such is the popular app Lose It. After setting a goal weight and a timeline, users receive graphic feedback that helps them modify their behaviour. Other apps have gone further still and make use of punishment. One example is GymPact. This app, as described in a feature article in *The Atlantic*,

> asks users to commit to visiting a gym a certain number of times each week and agree to forfeit at least $5 each time they skip. The app confirms users' presence at their gym via GPS and charges their credit card if they don't show up as planned. The company then divvies up the skip fees among those who honor their weekly commitments – so you get reinforced for going, and punished for not going.[49]

But then there are other, more advanced programs which extend beyond the screen of the phone. One example is Retrofit, which focuses on behavioural change. This program is described in the same *Atlantic* article: 'Retrofit users track their eating and exercise online and have weekly Skype sessions with a registered dietician, a psychologist, and a mind-set coach.... After the year is up, clients can still arrange occasional consultations, and Retrofit continues to monitor their weight via wireless scale, so that a coach can reach out if the number starts to rise.'

If it appears strange that self-trackers willingly submit themselves to this neo-authoritarianism, even paying money to be haunted by an external agency, then consider the even more paradoxical relation they seem to have to data and information. While happily sharing data about their bodies and daily behaviours, they violently protest about the way governments collect and store data. The former National Security Agency worker and whistle-blower Edward Snowden, himself a committed libertarian, is a celebrated hero among web evangelists for revealing the extent to which US governments spy not just on potential enemies, but also on their own allies and people. Trapped in an Orwellian fear, they see the government as a monstrous institution that spies on its own citizens.

The fear is exclusively fixed on paternal governments and their sister institutions, all of which, if you ask the libertarians, are designed to limit people's freedom. Meanwhile, little is said about the corporations, which, for a long time and in a relatively undisturbed fashion, have collected huge amounts of data. What make corporations such as Google and Facebook so valuable are not the services they provide but the data they possess, which they then use to help advertisers target potential customers. A corporation like Axciom, for example, collects huge amounts of data and is said to have records on hundreds of millions of Americans. Processing these data allows the company to label people according to a set of predefined categories, such as 'McMansions and Minivans' and 'adult with wealthy parents'.[50] Famously, a teenage girl was sent coupons for car seats and nappies. The girl's father complained to the company, accusing them of encouraging teen pregnancy. When he later found out that his daughter was in fact pregnant, he called back to apologize. She hadn't told anyone, but her consumption pattern had revealed the secret.

What are the implications of giving away personal data to corporations, and how are they likely to use this information in the future? In *Black Mirror*, a British television series of dystopian dramas, we find an uncanny answer. The young and disillusioned Bingham 'Bing' Madsen lives in a huge anonymous complex; what the anthropologist Marc Augé would call a non-place.[51] His tiny room, a futuristic version of a dormitory cell, consists of only one bed, surrounded by four LCD walls. Like a television that can't be switched off, these walls light up and play personally tailored commercials. One of the most frequently appearing is for a soft porn show called *Wraith Babes*. These commercials appear

throughout the complex, wherever there are screens, including the public toilet and the canteen. When Bing runs into
a woman whom he is attracted to in the public toilet, they
are interrupted by the sudden appearance of a *Wraith Babes*
advertisement, revealing Bing's secret viewing habits.

This is a society of control. Every small step and every
daily activity is recorded, which determines your personal
merit point, always visible at the top of your screen. The
merit points are used to pay for food in vending machines,
to get toothpaste on your brush, to watch films or to play
popular games. To gain points, Bing and the other citizens
living in the complex spend their day in the gym, wearing
grey track-suits. From morning to evening they cycle on
exercise bikes – which generates the electricity for the infinite
number of LCD screens around them. While on their cycles
collecting points, they can choose to watch movies or play
games or just watch their 'doppel' avatar cycling along an
artificial countryside road. (This inevitably evokes the image
of the bicycle desk, where people work, exercise and produce
energy at the same time.)

What this drama captures is the circular existence of the
precariat, who work long hours with no sense of purpose,
and no opportunity of upward mobility. The points that they
gain from a full day of cycling are enough to get by: to buy
food and consume some escapist entertainment in their
room. It should be noted that they are not the worst off. The
obese are lower in rank and are left to clean up in the
complex, while receiving constant abuse. For the cycling
precariat, life is an extended experience of boredom intensified by cheap entertainment. The only avenue to change your
life, and to break away from an uncertain existence trapped
in the complex, is to land an audition on *Hot Shots*, an
X-Factor-style game show. This is an option only for the
few, because it costs 15,000,000 points, a sum that could
take a lifetime to accumulate.

One should recall here that internships, which are often
a necessary route to escape the precariat, are now sold at

auctions. As Andrew Ross has observed, 'A Versace intern-
ship fetched $5000 at auction, temporary blogging rights at
the *Huffington Post* went for $13,000, and someone paid
$42,500 for a one-week stint at *Vogue*.'[52]

This takes us back to the opening discussion of this
chapter. As a professional jobseeker you are thrown into a
game, not by choice but by necessity. It is very difficult to
work out for whose pleasure this game is constructed. It
certainly isn't for the players themselves, who are kept in
constant suspense, thrown between hope and despair. 'Job
seekers must continue to believe that each time they apply
for a job they stand a real chance of "winning,"' Ofer
Sharone writes.[53] This adds an unexpected twist to the ideology of choice. Finding a job is about choice and personal
effort: if we work hard enough, both on our CV and on our
attitude, we will finally get what we are looking for. But this
is not the full story. What we need, in addition, is luck.

This paradoxical relationship between chance and choice
defines the reality of the neoliberal agent. To see how this
works in practice, consider how corporations have started
to use games in their search for appropriate recruits. The
small Silicon Valley start-up Knack offers a range of app-
based video games to improve the hiring process. One of
them is the quest game Dungeon Scrawl, and another is
Wasabi Waiter, where the player is taking orders at a crowded
sushi restaurant. 'These games aren't just for play,' the journalist Don Peck points out in *The Atlantic*: 'They've been
designed by a team of neuroscientists, psychologists, and
data scientists to suss out human potential.'[54] According to
Knack's founder, Guy Halfteck, twenty minutes of game
play is enough to generate a 'high-resolution of your psyche
and intellect, and an assessment of your potential as a leader
or an innovator'.

This means that the appropriate candidate is someone
with hidden faculties, which cannot be discerned through
normal techniques such as interviews or other tests. Instead,
the true talent can be spotted by how he or she plays a video

game. Interestingly, this intensifies the ambiguity. Before the game is played, neither the employer nor the candidate knows who the right person is.

What is at stake here is a move from an ideology of choice to an ideology of the chosen. 'All of us are doomed to the life of choices,' Zygmunt Bauman remarked, 'but not all of us have the means to be the choosers.'[55] In the current neoliberal constellation, where precarity meets the talent mindset, this has to be reversed. Today, not all of us have the means to be the chosen. This is the future of choice: while there is no guarantee that you will ever be chosen, you still have the chance, provided you start by paying the 15,000,000 merit points to appear on a talent show or the $42,500 for a stint at *Vogue*.

The harsh economic realities of the great talent lottery create some serious existential problems for the wo/men of now. After all, these are people who believe they can be anything, anytime. But the reality is far more constrained: they can only become themselves if they happen to be chosen in the great talent show that is otherwise known as the labour market.

5

Wellness, Farewell

To hell with health.[1]

Ivan Illich

The Freedom of the Sick-Bed

Normally we think about a sports injury as something of an inconvenience. This is not the case for the central character in Karl Ove Knausgaard's epic six-volume autobiographical novel *My Struggle*. During his weekly football match, Karl Ove breaks his collar-bone. On his return home from the emergency clinic, he describes the unlikely pleasure this unfortunate turn of events brings:

> After eating I lay down on the sofa with a cushion behind my back watching an Italian football match on TV. In the four years since we'd had children I had only done something like this once. At the time I was so ill I couldn't move, I lay on the sofa for a whole day, saw ten minutes of the first Jason Bourne film, slept for a bit, threw up intermittently, and even though my whole body ached and basically it was absolutely unbearable, I still enjoyed every second. Lying on the sofa and watching a film in the middle of the day! Now I had

that same feeling. I was *not* in a position to do anything. However much my shoulder burned and stung and ached, the pleasure at being able to lie in total peace was greater.[2]

Injuries and sickness are an inevitable part of life, and usually perceived as a misfortune. What Knausgaard does so brilliantly here is to disclose one of our shared guilty secrets: being incapacitated might be an inconvenience, but it is far better than dealing with the demands we face every day like working, tending to chores at home and of course looking after ourselves. Being violently ill or injured are the only two moments in four years when Karl Ove feels any sense of relief. Being ill releases him from the daily demands and finally allows him to live. For Knausgaard, true living does not seem to be found in being active or going out of his way to maximize his health and happiness. Instead, it is in moments of passivity and surrender that he begins to enjoy himself.

We find a remarkably similar sentiment expressed in a short autobiographical text by Rob Lucas. Describing his job as a web developer, Lucas notes how work begins to infiltrate ever more aspects of his life, including his dreams. Asking himself when he might find respite, all he can think of is when he gets ill. He writes that 'it is only when sickness comes and I am involuntarily rendered incapable of work that I really regain any extra time for myself. It is a strange thing to rejoice at the onset of flu with the thought that, in the haze of convalescence, one may finally be able to catch up with things pushed aside by work.'[3] For Lucas, the flu is a secret 'weapon' with which he might win some of his life back – at least for a day or two. The illness, he continues, is 'not wielded by a supposed aggressor'. It is not 'merely pathological, a contingency imposed on the body from without'. Rather, his illness feels 'almost willed – a holiday that the body demands for itself'.

To think of illness as an escape from the ever-present demands of work – or indeed normal life more generally – is by no means the preserve of post-industrial creative workers like Knausgaard and Lucas. It has far deeper historical roots. In *Illness as Metaphor*, Susan Sontag shows how, during the nineteenth and early twentieth century, tuberculosis (TB) sufferers were routinely represented as passionate, sexy, sensitive, interesting and creative. They were all the things nineteenth-century bourgeois society was not. By contracting TB, it was assumed that you could escape from the demands of respectable society: 'The TB sufferer was a dropout, a wanderer in endless search of a healthy place. Starting in the early nineteenth century, TB became a new reason for exile, for a life that was mainly travelling.'[4] Respite could only be found in beautiful and isolated places such as the mountains and deserts, the South Sea Islands and the Mediterranean. TB came to be seen not just as a horrible disease (which it undoubtedly was), but as 'a way of retiring from the world without having to take responsibility for the decision'.[5] Nowhere is this better illustrated, Sontag thinks, than in Thomas Mann's *The Magic Mountain*. In this novel, Hans Castorp, a solid young burgher of Hamburg, visits a friend at a sanatorium in the Swiss Alps for a few weeks. After receiving a rather spurious diagnosis, he stays for seven years to enjoy the mountain air and absence of responsibility, and engage in lengthy philosophical discussions with interesting companions. Perhaps this is the retreat that both Knausgaard and Lucas dream of. In their sickness-induced haze they see themselves escaping to their own Magic Mountain.

Checking out of life for seven years is not really an option for most office workers. In fact, being away for only a few days could attract suspicion. Taking sick leave for unjustified purposes (such as going Christmas shopping, recovering from a hangover or enjoying a beautiful sunny day) has become taboo. A recent study even suggests that as many as 74 per cent of us turn up to work even when we *are* sick.[6] While perhaps fantasizing about an escape to our own Magic Mountain, most of us continue to appear productive, despite the protests of our bodies.

Some employers have adopted a more accommodating approach and now acknowledge the need for an odd day off. By offering 'duvet days' (voluntary holidays that employees can take at short notice when they do not feel like coming into the office), these employers seek to cut back on the number of unwarranted 'sickies' which employees would otherwise take. One adventure clothing manufacturer has taken the practice a step further by using clandestine sick days as part of its advertising campaign.[7] In one of the company's catalogues it includes a chart showing the relation between one employee's absence from work and the size of the waves at a local beach. The employee was a keen surfer.

The attraction of illness lies in its capacity to redeem one of the greatest vices of our society: not doing anything. It is only when the body goes on strike that we are allowed to leave the workplace, not visit the gym or skip a session with our life coach. Sickness allows us to clock off, at least for a moment. What would otherwise appear as mere laziness now assumes the more acceptable form of respite. By surrendering to our illness, we are both following and reversing one of the central commands of biomorality – 'listen to your body'. As both Knausgaard and Lucas show us, this surrendering opens up a temporary space where the ill person can momentarily feel free from the burdens of responsibility. In the sick-bed we are allowed to pursue our own fancies, no matter how lazy and debased. But this only lasts for a short moment. While Hans Castorp in *The Magic Mountain* was able to remain at the sanatorium for seven years, the postmodern office worker usually only has a few days before his or her illness becomes seen as a problem.

Someone recovering from an illness might be given a degree of leeway. But if that person is seen as 'unmotivated to become healthy' or 'refusing to get better', then that is quite another matter. The assumption here is that illness is not mere happenstance. Rather, it is something which is self-created, something we are at least partly responsible for. This is a longstanding assumption, which Sontag traces back to the late nineteenth-century physician Georg Groddeck, who declared 'the sick man himself creates his disease.'[8] Another early physician, Karl Menninger, makes a similar case by claiming that 'illness is in part what the world has done to a victim, but in a large part it is what the victim has done with his world, and with himself.'[9] At the time of writing *Illness as Metaphor*, Sontag was herself undergoing treatment for cancer. She noticed that people around her would express similar views. For her, these 'preposterous and dangerous views manage to put the onus of the disease on the patient', where 'cure is thought to depend principally on the patient's already sorely tested or enfeebled capacity for self-love.'[10]

In a more recent study, Barbara Ehrenreich found remarkably similar sentiments among diagnosed cancer patients. On one breast cancer website she found positive affirmations such as: 'Don't cry over anything that can't cry over you'; 'When life hands out lemons, squeeze out a smile'; 'Don't wait for your ship to come in...swim out to meet it.' She also notes how a celebrity with cancer declares: 'cancer was the best thing that ever happened to me' and ' the source of my happiness was, of all things, cancer.' One book she comes across even describes cancer as a 'gift'.[11]

Although this language appears more positive than what we find in Groddeck and Menninger, the message is practically the same: even if patients are not responsible for developing cancer, they are responsible for the outcome. Some positive thinkers take a more cautious approach and say that while we might not choose the disease, we choose how we experience it. If we choose to confront it in a positive and upbeat way, we can regain a sense of control and agency. If we surrender and give up, we are to blame when the illness takes a turn for the worse.

Rather than creating an escape from the wellness command, illness might actually do the opposite. It may create a universe where the ill individual is dragged back into the imperative to become well again. It is no longer good enough for patients to rest. They must work on their health by thinking positively, participating in support groups, enduring special diets, and much more. Illness might temporarily liberate us from work, but it certainly does not liberate us from working on wellness. The result is that being sick becomes yet another full-time job with appointments to attend, health goals to meet and correct attitudes to foster.

Fat Acceptance

In Las Vegas, there is a place where wellness is certainly not on the menu: a scandalous restaurant called the Heart Attack Grill. On their website they boast: 'Ours is the only diet program in America that works.' As you walk into the restaurant you are greeted by one of the slim waitresses wearing a porn-inspired nurse uniform. She will help you get into a patient's robe and attach a wristband around your arm. The menu offers single-, double-, triple- and quadruple-bypass burgers. Customers over 350 pounds eat for free. When done with your meal – knowing that this was not exactly what your doctor had advised – you are offered a short spanking routine from one of the nurses (to relieve your sense of guilt, we may assume). Their website lists videos of shameful Americans being spanked after their calorie bonanza. And true enough, the diet seems to work. On 11 February 2012, a customer died from a heart attack while enjoying the triple-bypass burger. A year later another scandal erupted: a former hostess revealed that she was asked to film an unconscious customer so they could send it to the media.[12]

The Heart Attack Grill offers us an inverted image of the wellness command. It does not encourage customers to listen to their bodies, carefully monitor their calorie intake and create a healthy self. Instead, customers are encouraged to forget their bodies, ignore dietary advice and lust after unhealthiness. A similar message can be found in Richard Klein's postmodern anti-diet book, *Eat Fat*. He briefly contemplates how such an anti-diet could be achieved. 'Go on a diet and eat only grease?' For Klein, an all-fat diet might be one way out of the impossible demands of being slim and healthy. Fat, Klein argues, is a 'visible sign that in crucial areas of our life we have failed to be all we could be. An inescapable source of disappointment, of sadness and guilty self-contempt – of unrelenting shame.'[13]

The Heart Attack Grill turned this celebration of fat into a PR stunt, but others have tried to take this pro-fat message much more seriously. In Irmgard Tischner's *Fat Lives* we meet overweight women who adhere to social norms in public by eating correctly, but rebel in the privacy of their own homes by eating what they want.[14] For them, eating is not about satiating hunger. It is a way of resisting the slim norms they find so oppressive. This calorific militancy is not just individual in scope. The Fat Acceptance movement have sought to reclaim the dignity of the fat by placing fatness within the pale of bourgeois respectability. Groups like the National Association to Advance Fat Acceptance (NAAFA) have evoked the civil rights agenda to advance equality, end discrimination and empower the overweight. They compare the plight of the overweight with other minority groups. Their mission statement declares: 'Millions of fat Americans...constitute a minority group with many of the attributes of other minority groups: poor self-image, guilt feelings, employment discrimination, exploitation by commercial interests, and being the subject of ridicule.' Campaigns are mounted to protect the dignity of the overweight. For instance, the Bay Area group ran a successful campaign to have billboards discriminating against fat people removed from the city. The association has also sought to support legal measures aimed at curtailing discrimination on the basis of weight. But one of the major focuses of the movement's activities seems related to lifestyle issues. In her study of the movement, Anne Kirkland reports that the association's annual conference included many sessions on fitness, arts and craft, personal care, travel and sexuality.[15] Courses were offered on 'water aerobics', 'reclaiming the power to love ourselves', 'men who love fat women' and 'everything you wanted to know about fat sex but were afraid to ask'. When interviewing members of the Fat Acceptance movement, Kirkland noticed that they were eager to display other positive characteristics, such as being good at one's job.

What is striking with the Fat Acceptance movement is that, in failing to meet the criteria of a particular body-type, they seek to gain legitimacy and respect by drawing on notions of wellbeing (you can be fat and still be healthy) and other characteristics associated with an active life (being socially outgoing, hard-working and adventurous). Many of the people Kirkland interviewed emphasized their positive mindset and active orientation. For instance, one plus-sized beauty queen explained that 'if there was job discrimination I think it was mostly in my own head. And I say that because where I am now with it is that I'm bright, I have the talent, I'll show you that I have the talent and I'm bright. And if you don't want to hire me, well I don't want to be there. Which is pretty empowered.'[16] A similar upbeat approach can be seen on the Fat Acceptance blog Two Whole Cakes. One entry proclaims: 'Damn y'all, how busy have I been? Really, really busy!' This is not a fat and lazy person, worthy of condemnation. This is the woman of now, who proudly vocalizes all of the values associated with the wellness syndrome except one: slimness. This points to a problem that Richard Klein identifies with the Fat Acceptance movement: 'Acceptance often means resignation, a reluctant willingness to accept what one cannot change but deep down would still love to.' He continues: 'Fat acceptance demands tolerance from others but often continues to share the general hatred of fat in the form of self-hatred.'[17]

The acceptance of fat becomes a re-articulation of the same ideology the overweight seek to resist. The reasoning seems to be: I may be fat, but I am resilient, outgoing, positive and express my individuality, hence I am worthy of (some) respect. In this sense, the Fat Acceptance movement largely subscribe to the same notions of wellness that relentlessly underscore health and happiness. They just seek to tweak the perception of the body so that a bigger body-size can also fall within the domain of acceptable wellness. Participants are reminded that they can exercise, enjoy an active sex life and enter a beauty contest no matter what their size. To give up the battle of being slim, proponents of Fat Acceptance suggest, one should work harder on all other fronts by being more active, more networked and more interesting.

Bug-Chasing

In addition to shirking work and over-indulging in food, risky sex has been used to resist the demands of wellness. Perhaps one of the most interesting sexual practices to chart an escape route from wellness in recent years is 'barebacking', which involves gay men having sex without condoms. What makes barebacking fascinating is that it calls into question the ethic of wellness through unsafe sex. In his book *Unlimited Intimacy*, Tim Dean explores this culture. 'Rather than mindless fucking,' he explains, 'bareback sex is an activity deeply invested with meaning.'[18] The bareback community is roughly divided into two groups. First we have the 'bug-chasers', for whom the HIV virus is a central erotic component. They wish to receive it, ideally again and again, which they can do only by not testing themselves for the virus and imagining that, for every new sexual encounter, they are being 'bred' or handed the 'gift' (receiving HIV). And then we have the 'gift-givers' (men with HIV who are willing to share it), who are fewer in numbers and less open, partly because deliberately spreading the virus is, in legal terms, a criminal activity. Gift-givers are typically ultra-male figures, sometimes adorned with 'war scars' which reveal they carry the virus.

Barebacking cuts directly against the imperatives of wellness we have charted in earlier chapters. Unsurprisingly, it has inspired a sense of shock in both the straight as well as

the mainstream gay press. But Dean argues that to understand the significance of barebacking, we need to place it in
the context of the AIDS epidemic, after which homosexuals
became viewed with even more suspicion than before. To
rebalance this view, one of the central strategies was to
advance an image of the male homosexual as sexually
responsible. This meant being abstinent or engaging only in
'safe sex'. Unprotected anal sex became a strict taboo, not
just for individual couples, but also for the porn industry,
which took its educational role seriously.

The problem with this, Dean points out, is that the sani-
tization of the homosexual was the same as 'desexualizing
gayness, downplaying kinkiness, and pathologizing the
sexual subcultures, including barebacking, that queers have
invented'.[19] In short, it was a political process by which
homosexuals would be educated into respectable citizens.
Bareback culture became a rejection of these values. By
directly confronting the command to be safe and stay healthy,
barebacking invents new sexual identities. Instead of trying
to win widespread legitimacy, it seeks to develop a practice
beyond norms of healthiness and careful sexual risk management. By bringing danger back into the sexual encounter,
and by making each encounter into a potential life-and-
death moment, it adds a degree of gravity to sexuality.
It makes sex into a form of enjoyment beyond safe moderation. This is achieved through the constant reminder that
fucking is not just part of optimizing your health. It can
indeed kill you.

More than just providing an unsanitized, unlimited and
potentially deadly form of enjoyment, Dean argues, practices
of barebacking also tie men together in a new mode of intimacy. Through the HIV virus, men create a kind of lineage,
a filial relationship which they must carry with them throughout their lives. It creates a kinship network, a genealogy of
sorts, which allows men to create connections between and
across generations. Straight genealogies might work on the
basis of who gave birth to whom. It is no surprise then that
barebackers talk about passing on the virus as 'breeding'.

What makes this subculture particularly interesting with regard to biomorality is the fact that it deliberately rejects an ideology of individual wellness. More than that, it openly questions the image of the well-nurtured body as one that could live forever. It betrays the axiomatic values of wellness. The power of this approach, Dean suggests, lies in its capacity to evade 'superegoistic health imperatives'. It becomes a way to 'express skepticism regarding ideals of health and risk-avoidance, and to learn to live with mortality'.[20]

Few would resist the wellness command in a more concrete manner than barebackers. They are not just avoiding the imperatives of being healthy and normal; they are inverting these demands and throwing them back at society in a way that shocks and unsettles prevailing moral norms. They are not apologetic in the same manner as the fat who secretly seek to master other aspects of wellness. With regard to health, barebackers resolutely reject the wellness command. Yet they seem to remain intimately connected to one particular aspect of the wellness syndrome: the pursuit to become authentic. When confronting death in a heroic manner, they embody a particular vision of the authentic self. War scars are used to distinguish their own unique selves from those of the masses. Their sexual athleticism is constantly evaluated in relation to those of others. Like the wo/man of now, the search for new pioneering expressions of the self continues. New depths are explored. Pursuing authenticity, expressing one's own individuality, distinguishing oneself from others and developing one's networking skills – these are all vital aspects of the self-work that we find in the wellness syndrome. It is the labour on our selves which, in spite of being pitched against wellness, risks tying us closer to the very ideology we seek to escape. While barebackers present an intriguing resistance to health imperatives, they may be struggling to escape the demand to actualize themselves, a demand which rests on the pernicious illusion that one day we will win our true authentic selves. As long as we hold on to that notion, the wellness syndrome will hold on to us, keeping us in a firm grip.

Conclusion

To happiness in the strict sense, we may prefer pleasure, as a brief moment of ecstasy stolen in the course of things, gaiety, the lighthearted drunkenness that accompanies life's development, and especially joy, which presupposes surprise and elation.

Pascal Bruckner, *Perpetual Euphoria*, 2010[1]

In early 2013, *The New York Review of Books* published an article by the novelist Zadie Smith, called 'Joy'. For some readers, this might have seemed slightly out of tune with the magazine's other material. Amid long and serious musings on the Italian painter Raphael's late period and a specialized review of recent work on the inner life of birds, readers found Smith's personal account of a drug-infused night spent dancing in a club. The significance of this night, described in great detail even though it occurred almost two decades ago, is that it brought Smith close – terrifyingly close – to what she describes as joy, 'that strange admixture of terror, pain, and delight'.[2]

Joy, as Bruckner argues above, presupposes surprise and elation. But it also has a disruptive and ravaging effect. It takes us in a firm grip, and shakes us brutally. Perhaps it is a good thing, then, that joy is a rare emotional experience.

As Smith remarks: 'If you asked me if I wanted more joyful experiences in my life, I wouldn't be at all sure I did, exactly because it proves such a difficult emotion to manage.'

What lends joy its distinct character is that it goes beyond pleasure. We know from Freud that pleasure and excess are not compatible. The entire idea behind the pleasure principle is that it should regulate our intake of pleasure as a diabetic regulates his or her sugar level. Too much pleasure is bad news; it means we will soon have to pay the price of pain. When seeking pleasure, we also try to dodge displeasure. This demands determination, hard work and a sense of moderation. You can have a burger, as long as it is the healthy, organic type, made of grass-fed beef, and you go for a run afterwards. Doing this optimizes your happiness and health, and demonstrates that you are a conscious and caring person at the same time.

We are offered these measured pleasures constantly: decaffeinated coffee, safe sex, fat-free chocolate, sugar-free soft drinks and environmentally friendly SUVs. It would not be entirely surprising if drug cartels are currently developing a brand of fairly traded cocaine.

Our society offers an excess of measured pleasures. Joy, however, is rare. Zadie Smith recalls that, in the course of her life, she has encountered joy five or perhaps six times. Some of these occasions involved love: extraordinary moments when the boring external world would melt away. In the company of a special person, reality would take on a new shape. In those moments, nothing would seem more alien than to try to control and regulate your joy. When little else seems to matter, we don't shy away from potential danger. When Smith and her then lover are stuck in the grounds of a museum, they contemplate whether they should spend the night sleeping on a stone lion or jump from a high wall and break their ankles. No signs of agony. No concerns about danger. Just joy.

Yet it is not the transformative experience of love that Smith describes most vividly in her piece. It is that drug-infused experience which took place at the Fabric night club, close to the old Smithfields meat market in London. It is described as a full night out, memorable in every sense of the word, with the kind of music everyone already knew yet in that moment felt as if they were hearing for the very first time. The drugs kicked in and the music intensified. Men without shirts and women wearing strange tops that looked rather like aprons were united on the floor. Everybody danced. It was a special night, a night of joy.

'Fellow Britons!', she writes. 'Those of you, that is, who were fortunate enough to take the first generation of the amphetamine ecstasy and yet experience none of the adverse, occasionally lethal reactions we now know others suffered – yes, for you people I have a question. Was that Joy?' Smith is not entirely sure, but it was a night to remember – that's indisputable. She describes how she was absorbed in a float-ing world of chemically like-minded people. She recalls how, while she was lost in the music, 'a rail-thin man with enor-mous eyes reached across a sea of bodies for my hand. I took the man's hand. The top of my head flew away. We danced and danced. We gave ourselves over to joy.' She can't remem-ber the name of this fellow raver, but calls him Smiley. *You feeling it?*, was the line he kept repeating. *You feeling it yet?* His entire organism seemed directed to her experience, and determined that she should *feel* it.

Joy is something different from pleasure. 'A beach holiday is pleasure,' Smith argues. 'But on that dance floor I *was* joy.'

Smith realized all too quickly that this joy was not sustain-able. The moment she woke up, she found that Smiley was no longer a 'jester spirit-animal saviour person', but had become 'a crushingly boring skinny pill head, already smoking a joint, who wanted to borrow twenty quid for a cab'. She quickly came to doubt that this night, this moment when 'Can I Kick It?' mixed into 'Smells like Teen Spirit', had really been joy at all. Maybe it was just a contrivance of chemicals.

It is the impermanence of this moment that gives it weight and meaning. Unlike the easily replaceable everyday pleasure, joy is something that comes unexpectedly, and leaves in the same way. It cannot easily be repeated, replicated and brought back to life. Joy dies. And attempts to resuscitate it only leave us with a hollow shell. For Smith, it is precisely our realization that, one day, this experience will go away that makes it so much more important than any measured and repeatable pleasure.

Two decades after Smith's nocturnal adventures, a new club, located not far from Fabric, has opened up. The club is known as Morning Glory. Here, drugs are strictly banned; and so is alcohol. Not just that, all forms of excessive enjoyment are absent. Hundreds of city workers come here early in the morning to dance to deep house club anthems.[3] 'It's like clubbing, but instead of crawling out into the darkness afterwards feeling horrible, you go to work feeling great,' one of the organizers explains. 'And instead of having a beer you have coffee, a croissant and a massage.'[4]

Morning Glory is a club designed to improve your health, maximize your wellness and prepare you for a long and productive day at work. It is the obligatory hangout of the wo/men of now who want to rave themselves into the day. Here, you will not run into spaced-out boys, like Smiley, Smith's skinny pill head. You are more likely to meet the life-logger who keeps a detailed record of his wife's menstrual cycle.

Morning Glory is not a place of joy. It's a place ruled by measured pleasure. All forms of excess are carefully avoided, except, perhaps, extravagant sports clothes in ironically bright colours. What makes Morning Glory so contemporary is its ability to marry the pleasure principle with the broader obligation to be a productive wellness maximizer. It is the place for the fun-loving, extroverted and vocalizing individual who loves to work and party, especially when the two are combined.

Becoming a wo/man of now requires endless self-work: waking up early in the morning to dance oneself into a productive mood, taking mindfulness classes to become more focused, and monitoring one's career goals with a life coach. Such elaborate techniques, dedicated to enhancing the body, are not just triggered by a deep loyalty to pleasure. They are also activated by the uncertainties of the market, looming over the neoliberal agent as a foreboding cloud. Remember Dancy, the unemployed man who reshaped himself through meticulous self-tracking? For him, self-tracking was not used primarily for his own pleasure, as a path towards greater happiness and better health. It was a way to make him more desirable in an increasingly competitive labour market.

Dancy is remarkably loyal to the wellness command. Self-tracking regulates his entire life, with regard to both pleasure and work. He combines the pleasure principle with the rule of the market, mixing pleasure with business. If long walks yield pleasure, then why not install a treadmill under your desk? Injecting oneself with a steady stream of pleasure prolongs one's ability to work longer and more effectively, to stay concentrated at one's desk. The same goes for meetings: why lock oneself up into a room when one can perform better outdoors, in a walking meeting? Those in the workplace who have not yet taken these lessons to heart – who have failed to understand the ethics of making themselves healthier and more productive – will be offered membership of a health programme. If that doesn't work, they will be sentenced to a private session with a life coach.

While the wellness command is intimately attached to the contemporary work ethic, it is by no means confined to the workplace. The line between life and work is increasingly difficult to draw. We have seen how life coaches don't just address our work personas; they seek to plumb our psychological depths. Private passions such as horse-riding have been turned into corporate instructional techniques. Getting a tattoo has become a way to express your allegiance to the company. Throughout this book we have documented how the wellness command seeps into all aspect of our lives, at all times. It transforms every conceivable activity, including eating, meditating and even sleeping, into an opportunity to optimize pleasure and become more productive.

And yet, as we have demonstrated in the course of this book, the more we concentrate on maximizing our wellness, the more alienated and frustrated we seem to become. The frantic search for the perfect diet; the paranoid pursuit of happiness; the forced workplace work-out; the endless life-coaching sessions; the detailed tracking of our bodily functions; turning your entire day into a game – these desperate attempts to increase productivity through wellness create their own problems. They encourage an infectious narcissism which pushes us to take the great turn inwards, making our body into our first and last concern. They generate a creeping sense of anxiety that comes with the ever-present responsibility of monitoring every lifestyle choice. They feed a sense of guilt that comes from the inevitable slip-ups when we don't follow our diet or fail to live up to our life goals. People whose life has been seized by wellness are not just healthier, happier and more productive. They are also narcissistic, anxious and guilty. They are victims of the wellness syndrome.

Biomorality does not just inflict its enthusiasts with personal pathologies; it reshapes how they engage with others. Those who don't live up to high standards of wellness are looked at with disgust. And as this vitriolic language becomes common in the public sphere, the possibility for reasoned debate fades. As authorities lose faith in structural reforms, they become more interested in small-scale behavioural interventions. In place of politics, we are left with corporeal babble and increasingly invasive lifestyle tweaks. As a result, we abandon political demands. The just redistribution of material resources (through 'social welfare'), the recognition of previously maligned identities (through 'identity politics') and the representation of political voices (through 'democratization') have now become replaced by a new ambition:

personal rehabilitation. Here, the unemployed are not provided with an income; they get life coaching. Discriminated groups don't get opportunities to celebrate their identities; they get an exercise plan. Citizens don't get the opportunity to influence decisions that affect their lives; they get a mindfulness session. Meanwhile, inequality, discrimination and authoritarianism become seen as questions too grand to tackle head-on. Instead, political ambitions become myopically focused on boosting our wellbeing.

This concern with rehabilitating our health and happiness has not gone unchallenged. It has sparked new forms of what Peter Fleming calls 'post-recognitional politics'.[5] These are political movements that challenge authority by checking out. The ill take to their bed, fat accepters get rid of the bathroom scales and barebackers avoid testing their HIV status. Each try to create a new way of experiencing the world unencumbered by the wellness command. This might open up new spaces of respite, but in doing so these anti-biomoral militants are often becoming even more tightly tied to their bodily obsessions.

The fate of these escape attempts reminds us that finding a way out of the wellness syndrome is not easy. But a start would be to stop obsessively listening to our bodies, to give up fixations with our own health and happiness and to abandon the illusion of limitless human potential. Instead we could forget about our bodies for a moment, stop chasing after happiness and realize that, as human beings, we are not just defined by our potential to be healthy and happy. Wellness is not always our lot.

To escape the clutches of wellness, we might recognize that, as humans, we are defined not exclusively by our potentials, but also by our impotence. And this is nothing to be ashamed of. Accepting our impotence allows us to see that we will always come up short in one way or another. What makes most important things in life worthwhile is the inevitable failures and pain they entail. Truth often makes us miserable. Political action may involve direct threats and danger. Beauty is often soaked in sorrow. Love usually tears us apart. They may hurt, but not more, as Smith points out, than they are worth.

'Why would anyone accept such a crazy deal?', Smith asks. 'Surely if we were sane and reasonable we would every time choose a pleasure over a joy, as animals themselves sensibly do. The end of a pleasure brings no great harm to anyone, after all, and can always be replaced with another of more or less equal worth.'[6] The really insane and unreasonable thing, we would argue, is to only accept and look for pleasure. For sure, this would minimize the travails of feeling unwell and optimize our happiness indicators. Yes, this might mean less pain, but it will also lead us into isolation. Instead of forever dwelling on our own sickness, we would do better to look at and act on the sickness of the world.

Notes

Introduction

1 Hervé Juvin, *The Coming of the Body* (London: Verso, 2010), p. 34.

2 These include: Duke, Texas A&M, Qunnipac, Loyola, North Dakota, North Carolina, East Carolina, UC Davis, Seattle, Clemson, Syracuse, American, Denver and Southern Florida.

3 Lancey Rose, 'The best places to go to prison', *Forbes*, 25 May 2006.

4 Jonathan M. Metzl, 'Introduction: Why "against health"?', in Jonathan M. Metzl and Anna Kirkland, eds, *Against Health: How Health Became the New Morality* (New York: New York University Press, 2010), p. 2.

5 Lauren Berlant, 'Risky bigness: On obesity, eating, and the ambiguity of "health"', in Metzel and Kirkland, eds, *Against Health*, p. 26.

6 As quoted in Berlant, 'Risky bigness', p. 26.

7 Will Davies, 'The political economy of unhappiness', *New Left Review*, 71, 2011, p. 65.

8 Alenka Zupančič, *The Odd One In* (Cambridge MA: MIT Press, 2008), p. 5.

9 Slavoj Žižek, *In Defense of Lost Causes* (London: Verso, 2008), p. 30.

10 Renata Salecl, *Choice* (London: Profile, 2010), p. 5.
11 Kim Severson, *Spoonfed: How Eight Cooks Saved My Life* (New York: Riverhead, 2010).
12 Pascal Bruckner, *Perpetual Euphoria: On the Duty to be Happy* (Princeton, NJ: Princeton University Press, 2010), p. 53.
13 Steven Poole, *You Aren't What You Eat* (London: Union, 2012).
14 Carl Elliott, *Better Than Well: American Medicine Meets the American Dream* (New York: W.W. Norton, 2003), p. 30.
15 Elliott, *Better Than Well*, p. 34.
16 Simon Critchley, *Infinitely Demanding: Ethics of Commitment, Politics of Resistance* (London: Verso, 2007), p. 4.

Chapter 1   The Perfect Human

1 Christopher Lasch, *The Culture of Narcissism: American Life in an Age of Diminished Expectations* (New York: W.W. Norton, 1979) , p. 4.
2 'Pursuit of Happiness radio show couple found dead in New York', *Guardian*, 7 June 2013.
3 Taffy Brodesser-Akner, 'The merchant of just be happy', *New York Times*, 28 December 2013.
4 Arlie Russell Hochschild, *The Outsourced Self: Intimate Life in Market Times* (New York: Metropolitan Books, 2012), pp. 219–28.
5 Marie Myung-Ok Lee, 'Want to be a better worker? Please consult this horse', *The Atlantic*, 2 September 2011.
6 Brodesser-Akner, 'The merchant of just be happy'.
7 Spencer Jones, 'Should a life coach have a life first?', *New York Times*, 27 January 2012.
8 Eve Tahmichioglu, 'Coaches wanted in the game of life', *New York Times*, 12 January 2008.
9 Brodesser-Akner, 'The merchant of just be happy'.
10 Arlie Russell Hochschild, 'The outsourced life', *New York Times*, 5 May 2012.
11 Salecl, *Choice*, p. 33.
12 Salecl, *Choice*, pp. 33–4.
13 Lasch, *The Culture of Narcissism*, p. 177.

14 Slavoj Žižek, *The Ticklish Subject: The Absent Centre of Political Ontology* (London: Verso, 2000), p. 368.
15 Žižek, *The Ticklish Subject*, p. 368.
16 Luc Boltanski and Eve Chiapello, *The New Spirit of Capitalism* (London: Verso, 2007).
17 Andrew Ross, *No Collar: The Humane Workplace and Its Hidden Costs* (Philadelphia: Temple University Press, 2003).
18 http://positivesharing.com/2006/10/10-seeeeeriously-cool-workplaces/.
19 Micha Solomon, 'The hazards of hiring like Zappos', *Forbes*, 5 March 2014.
20 Ivor Southwood. *Non-Stop Inertia* (Alresford, Hants: Zero, 2011), p. 20.
21 Southwood, *Non-Stop Inertia*, p. 1.
22 Southwood, *Non-Stop Inertia*, p. 3.
23 Salecl, *Choice*, p. 23.
24 Chade-Meng Tan, *Search Inside Yourself* (London: Collins, 2012).
25 Catlin Kelly, 'O.K. Google, Take a deep breath', *New York Times*, 28 April 2012.
26 Tan, *Search Inside Yourself*, p. 33.
27 Julie Watson, 'Marine Corps study how mindfulness meditation can affect troops', *Huffington Post*, 19 January 2013.
28 Ron Purser and David Loy, 'Beyond McMindfulness', *Huffington Post*, 7 January 2013.
29 Ben Goldacre, *Bad Science* (London: Harper Perennial, 2009).
30 Purser and Loy, 'Beyond McMindfulness'.
31 Karl E. Weick and Ted Putnam, 'Organizing for mindfulness: Eastern wisdom and Western knowledge', *Journal of Management Inquiry*, 15(3), 2006, p. 280.
32 Juvin, *The Coming of the Body*, p. xii.
33 A.G. Sultzberger, 'Hospitals shift smoking bans to smoker bans', *New York Times*, 10 February 2011.
34 Robert Proctor, *The Nazi War on Cancer* (Princeton, NJ: Princeton University Press, 2000), p. 173.
35 Lawrence O. Gostin, 'Global Regulatory Strategies for Tobacco Control' *Georgetown Law Faculty Publications*, Washington, 2007, Paper 481.

36 Joanne Brewis and Christopher Grey, 'The regulation of smoking at work', *Human Relations*, 61(7), 2008, pp. 965–87.
37 Chantal Mouffe, *On the Political* (London: Routledge, 1996), p. 5.
38 Salecl, *Choice*, p. 55.
39 Salecl, *Choice*, p. 55.

Chapter 2   The Health Bazaar

1 Richard Klein, *Eat Fat* (New York: Pantheon Books, 1996), p. 22.
2 Alexandra Michel, 'Transcending socialization: A nine-year ethnography of the body's role in organizational control and knowledge workers' transformation', *Administrative Science Quarterly*, 56(3), 2011, p. 339.
3 Michel, 'Transcending socialization', p. 339.
4 Michel, 'Transcending socialization', p. 339.
5 Michel, 'Transcending socialization', p. 341.
6 Michel, 'Transcending socialization', pp.342–3.
7 Michel, 'Transcending socialization', p. 354.
8 Jonathan Crary, *24/7: Late Capitalism and the Ends of Sleep* (London: Verso, 2013).
9 Jim Loehr and Tony Schwartz, 'The making of a corporate athlete', *Harvard Business Review*, 79(1), 2011, pp. 120–9
10 Loehr and Schwartz, 'The making of a corporate athlete', p. 122.
11 Loehr and Schwartz, 'The making of a corporate athlete', p. 128.
12 Soeren Matteke, Hangsheng Liu, John Caloyeras, et al., *Workplace Wellness Programs Study: Final Report* (Santa Monica, CA: RAND, 2013).
13 Olga Khazan, 'Employers tell workers to get a move on', *Los Angeles Times*, 15 May 2011.
14 World Economic Forum, *Working Towards Wellness* (2007).
15 Olga Khazan, 'Health begins at work', *The Atlantic*, 13 November 2013.
16 Nilofer Merchant, 'Sitting is the smoking of our generation', *Huffington Post*, 18 January 2013.

17 Kate Brateskier, 'Walking meetings: Why you should schedule a conference on the move', *Huffington Post*, 24 June 2013.

18 Peter Bowes, 'Treadmill desks: How practical are they?', *BBC News Magazine*, 30 January 2013: http://www.bbc.co.uk/news/magazine-21076461.

19 James Hamblin, 'The electricity generating bicycle-desk that would power the world', *The Atlantic*, 7 January 2014.

20 Matteke et al., *Workplace Wellness Programs Study*.

21 Jill R. Horwitz, Brenna D. Kelly and John DiNardo, 'Wellness incentives in the workplace: Cost savings through cost shifting to unhealthy workers', *Health Affairs*, 32(3), 2013, pp. 468–76.

22 Mikael Holmqvist and Christian Maravelias, *Managing Healthy Organizations: Worksite Health Promotion and the New Self-Management Paradigm* (London: Routledge, 2010), p. 79.

23 Holmqvist and Maravelias, *Managing Healthy Organizations*, p. 80.

24 Christian Maravelias, Torkild Thanem and Mikael Holmqvist, 'March meets Marx: The politics of exploitation and exploration in the management of life and labour', *Research in the Sociology of Organizations*, 37, 2013, p. 144.

25 Holmqvist and Maravelias, *Managing Healthy Organizations*, p. 118.

26 Zygmunt Bauman, *Liquid Modernity* (Cambridge: Polity, 1999), p. 78.

27 Bauman, *Liquid Modernity*, p. 78.

28 Tina Rosenberg, 'A big church: A small group health solution', *New York Times*, 10 November 2011.

29 Rosenberg, 'A big church'.

30 Michael Mosley and Mimi Spencer, *The Fast Diet* (London: Short Books, 2013).

31 Bryan S. Turner, 'The government of the body: Medical regimens and the rationalization of diet', *British Journal of Sociology*, 33(2), 1982, pp. 254–69.

32 Turner, 'The government of the body', p. 265.

33 Turner, 'The government of the body', p. 268.

34 Sandra Lee Bartey, *Femininity and Domination: Studies in the Phenomenology of Oppression* (London: Routledge, 1990), p. 66.

35 Cressida J. Heyes, 'Foucault goes to Weight Watchers', *Hypatia*, 21(2), 2006, p. 133.

36 David Vise and Mark Malseed, *The Google Story* (New York: Delacourt Books, 2005), p. 194.

37 Vise and Malseed, *The Google Story*, p. 197.

38 Nanna Mik-Meyer, 'Managing fat bodies: Identity regulation between public and private domains', *Critical Social Studies*, 10(2), 2008, p. 28.

39 Nanna Mik-Meyer, 'The imagined psychology of being overweight in a weight loss program', in Jaber F. Gubrium and Margaretha Järvinen, eds, *Turning Troubles into Problems: Clientization in Human Services* (Abingdon: Routledge, 2013).

40 Mik-Meyer, 'The imagined psychology of being overweight', p. 29.

41 Holmqvist and Maravelias, *Managing Healthy Organizations*, p. 113.

42 Holmqvist and Maravelias, *Managing Healthy Organizations*, p. 80.

43 Nikolas Rose, *The Politics of Life Itself* (Princeton, NJ: Princeton University Press, 2006), p. 6.

44 Torkild Thanem, 'I'll have a burger, but a healthier burger: Bio-politics and dynamics micro-assemblages of bio-political struggle in workplace health promotion', paper presented at Academy of Management, Annual Meeting, Montreal, 2010, p. 18.

45 Julia Gutham, 'Teaching the politics of obseity: Insights into neoliberal embodiment and contemporary politics', *Antipode*, 41(5), 2009, p. 1117.

46 Carol Sternhell, 'You'll always be fat, but fat can be fit', *Ms Magazine*, April 1985. p. 62.

47 Steve Myall, 'The real secret to weightloss success is keeping it simple', *Mirror*, 18 February 2013.

48 Bauman, *Liquid Modernity*, p. 67.

49 John Germov and Lauren Williams, 'Dieting women: Self surveillance and the body panopticon', in Jeffery Sobel and Donna Maura, eds, *Weighty Issues: Fatness and Thiness as Social Problems* (Hawthorne, NY: Aldine de Gryuter, 1999), p. 122.

50 Janneke Harting, Patricia van Assema and Nanne K. de Vries, 'Patients' opinions on health counseling in the Hartslag Limburg cardiovascular prevention project: Perceived quality,

satisfaction, and normative concerns', *Patient Education and Counseling*, 61(6), 2006, pp. 142–51.

51 Christopher Dewberry and Jane M. Ussher, 'Restraint and perception of body weight among British adults', *The Journal of Social Psychology*, 134(5), 2001, pp. 609–16.

52 A.S. Chamove, P.A.M. Graham and C.M. Wallis, 'Guilt and obsessive-compulsive traits in female dieters', *Journal of Human Nutrition and Dietetics*, 4(2), 1991, pp. 113–19.

53 Sigmund Freud, 'Civilization and Its Discontents', *The Standard Edition of the Complete Psychological Works of Sigmund Freud, Volume XX1, 1927–1931* (London: Vintage, 2001), p. 125.

54 Freud, 'Civilization and Its Discontents', p. 128.

55 Jason Glynos, 'Self-transgressive enjoyment as a freedom fetter', *Political Studies*, 56(3), 2008, pp. 679–704.

56 Pascal Bruckner, *The Tyranny of Guilt: An Essay on Western Masochism* (Princeton, NJ: Princeton University Press, 2010).

57 Philip Mirowski, *Never Let a Good Crisis Go to Waste* (London: Verso, 2013).

58 James Delingpole, 'A conspiracy against chavs? Count me in', *The Times*, 13 April 2006.

59 Owen Jones, 'Posh people are not a persecuted minority', Verso blog, 1 June 2011. http://www.versobooks.com/blogs/563-owen-jones-in-response-to-james-delingpole-posh-people-are-not-a-persecuted-minority.

60 Owen Jones, *Chavs: The Demonization of the Working Class* (London: Verso, 2011).

61 Bev Skeggs. 'The making of class and gender through visualizing moral subject formation', *Sociology*, 39(5), 2005, p. 965.

62 Germaine Greer, 'Long live the Essex girl', *Guardian*, 5 March 2001.

63 Skeggs, 'The making of class and gender through visualizing moral subject formation', p. 967.

64 Skeggs, 'The making of class and gender through visualizing moral subject formation', p. 974.

65 Tim Ross, 'Minister: Poor families are likely to be obese', *The Daily Telegraph*, 22 January 2013.

66 Imogen Tyler, ' "Chav mum, chav scum": Class disgust in contemporary Britain', *Feminist Media Studies*, 8(1), 2008, pp. 17–34.

67 George Orwell, *The Road to Wigan Pier* (London: Penguin, 1937/1986), p. 119.
68 Stephanie Lawler, 'Disgusted subjects: The making of middle-class identities', *The Sociological Review*, 53(3), 2005, p. 430.
69 David Hume, *A Treatise on Human Nature* (London: Penguin, 1739/1969), p. 462.
70 Jonathan Haidt, 'The emotional dog and its rational tail: A social intutionist approach to moral judgement', *Psychological Review*, 108(4), 2001, pp. 814–34.
71 Jonathan Haidt, Silvia Helena Koller and Maria G. Dias, 'Affect, culture, and morality, or is it wrong to eat your dog?', *Journal of Personality and Social Psychology*, 65(4), 1993, p. 617.
72 Ange-Marie Hancock, *The Politics of Disgust: The Public Identity of the Welfare Queen* (New York: New York University Press), 2004.
73 Mary Douglas, *Purity and Danger: An Analysis of Conceptions of Pollution and Taboo* (London: Routledge and Kegan Paul, 1966).
74 Giles Hattersley, 'We know what food the kids like, and it's not polenta', *Sunday Times*, 24 September 2006.
75 Megan Warin, 'Foucault's progeny: Jamie Oliver and the art of governing obesity', *Social Theory and Health*, 9(1), 2011, p. 24.
76 Laurie Ouellette and James Hay, 'Makeover television, governmentality and the Good Citizen', *Continuum: Journal of Media and Cultural Studies*, 22(4), 2008, p. 6.
77 Joanne Hollows and Steve Jones, ' "At least he's doing something": Moral entrepreneurship and individual responsibility in *Jamie's Ministry of Food*', *European Journal of Cultural Studies*, 13(3), 2010, pp. 307–22.
78 Warin, 'Foucault's progeny'.

Chapter 3 The Happiness Doctrine

1 Samuel Beckett, *Waiting for Godot* (London: Faber, 1953), p. 60.
2 Martin Seligman, *Authentic Happiness* (New York: Free Press, 2002), p. xi.

3 Zig Ziglar quotes, available at www.quoteswise.com.
4 Goldacre, *Bad Science*.
5 Barbara Ehrenreich, *Smile or Die: How Positive Thinking Fooled America and the World* (London: Granta, 2009).
6 Ehrenreich, *Smile or Die*, p. 74.
7 Ehrenreich, *Smile or Die*, p. 89.
8 Norman Vincent Peale, *The Power of Positive Thinking* (New York: Fireside, 1952).
9 Peale, *The Power of Positive Thinking*, p. 4.
10 Napoleon Hill and W. Clement Stone, *Success through a Positive Mental Attitude* (New York: Pocket Books, 1960).
11 Hill and Stone, *Success Through a Positive Mental Attitude*, p. 6.
12 Ivan Robertson and Cary L. Cooper, *Well-being: Productivity and Happiness at Work* (New York: Palgrave Macmillan, 2011), p. 4.
13 Zig Ziglar, *See You at the Top* (Gretna: Pelican, 1975), p. 52.
14 Deepak Chopra, *The Ultimate Happiness Prescription: 7 Keys to Joy and Enlightenment* (Chatham: Ebury Publishing, 2010), p. 45.
15 Russ Harriss, *The Happiness Trap: How to Stop Struggling and Start Living* (Boston: Trumpeter Books, 2007).
16 Nicola Phoenix, *Reclaiming Happiness: 8 Strategies for an Authentic Life and Greater Peace* (Forres: Findhorn Press, 2011), p. 10.
17 Phoenix, *Reclaiming Happiness*, p. 10.
18 Thomas Bien, *The Buddha's Way of Happiness* (Oakland, CA: New Harbinger Publications), p. 13.
19 Veronica Ray, *Choosing Happiness: The Art of Living Unconditionally* (Centre City, MN: Hazelden, 1991), p. 10.
20 Seligman, *Authentic Happiness*, p. 96.
21 Eric G. Wilson, *Against Happiness* (New York: Farrar, Straus and Giroux), p. 25.
22 Wilson, *Against Happiness*, p. 28.
23 Seligman, *Authentic Happiness*, p. 8.
24 Seligman, *Authentic Happiness*, p. 129.
25 Ehrenreich, *Smile or Die*, p. 153.
26 Ehrenreich, *Smile or Die*, p. 157.
27 Ehrenreich, *Smile or Die*, p. 158.
28 Cited in Matthew Stewart, 'The management myth', *Atlantic Monthly*, June 2006, p. 81.

29 Stewart, 'The management myth', p. 81.

30 Shawn Achor, *The Happiness Advantage: The Seven Principles of Positive Psycology That Fuel Success and Performance at Work* (New York: Virgin Books, 2010), p. 4.

31 Achor, *The Happiness Advantage*, p. 4.

32 Gerald E. Ledford, 'Happiness and productivity revisited', *Journal of Organizational Behavior*, 20(1), 1999, p. 26.

33 Ledford, 'Happiness and productivity revisited', p. 27.

34 As described in Daniel Kahneman and Alan B. Krueger, 'Developments in the measurement of subjective well-being', *Journal of Economic Perspectives*, 20(1), 2006, pp. 3–24.

35 Sigmund Freud, 'A difficulty in the path of psycho-analysis', *The Standard Edition of the Complete Psychological Works of Sigmund Freud, Volume XVII, 1917–1919* (London: Vintage, 2001), p. 141.

36 Giorgio Agamben, *Profanations* (New York: Zone Books, 2007), p. 20.

37 Bruckner, *Perpetual Euphoria*, p. 113.

38 PM Speech on Wellbeing, 25 November 2010: https://www.gov.uk/government/speeches/pm-speech-on-wellbeing.

39 Philip Brickman, Dan Coates and Ronnie Janoff-Bulman, 'Lottery winners and accident victims: Is happiness relative?', *Journal of Personality and Social Psychology*, 36(8), 1978, pp. 917–27.

40 Brickman et al., 'Lottery winners and accident victims', p. 925.

41 Personal Well-being in the UK, 2011/12 and 2012/13: http://www.ons.gov.uk/ons/rel/wellbeing/measuring-national-well-being/personal-well-being-in-the-uk–2012-13/sty-personal-well-being-in-the-uk.html/.

42 'ONS well-being report reveals UK's happiness ratings', BBC, 24 July 2012. http://www.bbc.co.uk/news/uk-politics-18966729.

43 Tracy McVeigh, 'David Cameron measuring "wrong type of happiness"', *Guardian*, 10 April 2011.

44 McVeigh, 'David Cameron measuring "wrong type of happiness"'.

45 Rhonda Byrne, *The Secret* (New York: Atria Books, 2006), p. ix.

46 Byrne, *The Secret*, p. ix.

47 Byrne, *The Secret*, p. 7.

48 Catherine Bennett, 'Only an idiot could take The Secret seriously. Yet Cameron seems to be following its tips to the letter', *Guardian*, 26 April 2007.
49 Byrne, *The Secret*, p. 6.
50 Ehrenreich, *Smile or Die*, p. 8.
51 As cited in Victoria Moore, 'It's become the fastest-selling self-help book ever, but is The Secret doing more harm than good?', *The Daily Mail*, 26 April 2007. Part of this quote is found in Ehrenreich, *Smile or Die*, p. 205.
52 Bruckner, *Perpetual Euphoria*, p. 3.
53 Bruckner, *Perpetual Euphoria*, p. 19.
54 Bruckner, *Perpetual Euphoria*, p. 18.
55 Zupančič, *The Odd One In*, p. 63.
56 Pierre Bourdieu, *The Social Structures of the Economy* (Cambridge: Polity, 2005), p. 185.
57 Lauren Berlant, *Cruel Optimism* (Durham, NC: Duke University Press, 2011).
58 Terry Eagleton, 'What would Rousseau make of our selfish age?', *Guardian*, 27 June 2012.
59 As cited in Simon Critchley, 'Happy like God', *The New York Times*, 25 May 2009.
60 Robert Nozick, *Anarchy, State and Utopia* (New York: Basic Books, 1974), p. 42.
61 Bruckner, *Perpetual Euphoria*, p. 34.
62 This example is from Bruckner, *Perpetual Euphoria*, p. 115.
63 Mark Fisher, *Capitalist Realism: Is there No Alternative?* (London: Zero Books, 2009).
64 David Gritten, 'Shame: Steve McQueen interview', *The Telegraph*, 14 January 2012.
65 Slavoj Žižek, *The Parallax View* (Boston: MIT Press, 2006), p. 310.
66 Žižek, *The Parallax View*, p. 311.

Chapter 4   The Chosen Life

1 Cited in Christopher Hitchens, *Hitch 22: A Memoir* (New York: Atlantic, 2010), p. 330.
2 Harry Freedman, 'Tips to help you stay positive while jobhunting', *Guardian*, 24 May 2013.

3 John Domokos, 'Jobcentres "tricking" people out of benefits to cut costs, says whistleblower', *Guardian*, 1 April 2011.

4 Domokos, 'Jobcentres "tricking" people out of benefits to cut costs, says whistleblower'.

5 John Domokos, 'Government admits Jobcentres set targets to take away benefits', *Guardian*, 8 April 2011.

6 Patrick Wintour and John Domokos, 'Leaked Jobcentre news-letter urges staff to improve on sanctions targets', *Guardian*, 25 March 2013.

7 John Domokos and Patrick Wintour, 'Jobcentre "scorecard" shows how areas are performing on stopping benefits', *Guardian*, 28 March 2013.

8 Domokos, 'Jobcentres "tricking" people out of benefits to cut costs, says whistleblower'.

9 Ofer Sharone, *Flawed System, Flawed Self: Job Searching and Unemployment Experiences* (Chicago: University of Chicago Press, 2014), p. 27.

10 Ronald W. McQuaid and Colin Lindsay, 'The concept of employability', *Urban Studies*, 42(2), 2005, pp. 197–219.

11 McQuaid and Lindsay, 'The concept of employability'.

12 Jamie Peck and Nikolas Theodore, 'Beyond "employability"', *Cambridge Journal of Economics*, 24(6), 2000, pp. 729–49.

13 'From welfare to workfare', *The Economist*, 27 July 2006.

14 Conor Burns, 'Margaret Thatcher's greatest achievement: New Labour', 11 April 2008: http://conservativehome.blogs.com/centreright/2008/04/making-history.html.

15 Sharone, *Flawed System, Flawed Self*, p. 39.

16 Duncan Mathison and Martha I. Finney, *Unlock the Hidden Job Market* (Upper Saddle River, NJ: FT Press, 2010), p. 150.

17 Mathison and Finney, *Unlock the Hidden Job Market*, p. 150.

18 Mathison and Finney, *Unlock the Hidden Job Market*, p. 150.

19 Sharone, *Flawed System, Flawed Self*, p.71.

20 Andrew Ross, *Nice Work If You Can Get It* (New York: New York University Press, 2010), p. 6.

21 Ross, *Nice Work If You Can Get It*, p. 5.

22 Southwood, *Non-Stop Inertia*, p. 59.

23 Lucy Tobin, 'Job hunting: Forget a CV, you need the X factor', *Guardian*, 11 December 2011.

24 Eigil Söderin, 'Välkommen till autionsamhället', *ETC*, 1 November 2011.

25 Malcolm Gladwell, 'The talent myth', *The New Yorker*, 22 July 2002.
26 Klint Finley, 'The quantified man: How an obsolete tech guy rebuilt himself for the future', *Wired Magazine*, 22 February 2013.
27 Finley, 'The quantified man'.
28 Gary Wolf: http://quanitifiedself.com/.
29 'Counting every moment', *The Economist*, 3 March 2012.
30 April Dembosky, 'Invasion of the body hackers', *Financial Times*, 10 June 2011.
31 Dembosky, 'Invasion of the body hackers'.
32 Mirowski, *Never Let a Serious Crisis Go to Waste*, p. 105.
33 Mirowski, *Never Let a Serious Crisis Go to Waste*, p. 108.
34 David Asprey, 'How self-tracking can up-grade your brain and body', *Narrative*: http://blog.getnarrative.com/2013/04/how-self-tracking-can-upgrade-your-brain-and-body/.
35 Tim Ferriss, *The 4 Hour Body: An Uncommon Guide to Rapid Fat-Loss, Incredible Sex and Becoming Super-Human* (New York: Crown, 2010).
36 Steven Poole, 'Why the cult of hard work is counter-productive', *New Statesman*, 11 December 2013.
37 Poole, 'Why the cult of hard work is counter-productive'.
38 Evgeny Morozov, *To Save Everything Click Here* (New York: Public Affairs, 2013), p. 273.
39 David Oakley, 'Hedge funds turn to psychology software to revolutionise trading', *Financial Times*, 15 September 2013.
40 Gilles Deleuze, 'Postscript on the societies of control', *October*, 59, 1992, pp. 3–7. p. 7.
41 Mark Moschel, 'The beginner's guide to quantified self (plus, a list of the best personal data tools out there': http://technori.com/2013/04/4281-the-beginners-guide-to-quantified-self-plus-a-list-of-the-best-personal-data-tools-out-there/.
42 Nikil Saval, 'The secret history of life-hacking', *Pacific Standard*, 22 April 2014.
43 Finley, 'The quantified man'.
44 Crary, 24/7, p. 46.
45 Susie Neilson, 'When a relationship becomes a game', *The Atlantic*, 8 August 2013.
46 Jemima Kiss, 'Turn chores into a game, with EpicWin', *Guardian*, 23 August 2010.

47 This is how Noam Chomsky put it in a talk, available on Youtube 'Noam Chomsky vs B.F. Skinner. See also Noam Chomsky, 'The Case Against B.F. Skinner', *The New York Review of Books*, 30 December 1971.

48 As cited in David H. Freedman, 'The perfected self', *The Atlantic*, 21 May 2012.

49 Freedman, 'The perfected self'.

50 Alice E. Marwick, 'Your data are being deeply mined', *The New York Review of Books*, 9 January 2014.

51 Marc Augé, *Non-Places: Introduction to an Anthropology of Supermodernity* (London: Verso, 1995).

52 Andrew Ross, 'A capitalist's dream', *London Review of Books*, 19 May 2011.

53 Ofer Sharone, 'Constructing unemployed job seekers as professional workers: The depoliticizing work-game of job searching', *Qualitative Sociology*, 30(4), 2007, p. 412

54 Don Peck, 'They're watching you at work', *The Atlantic*, 20 November 2013.

55 Zygmunt Bauman, 'The self in a consumer society', *The Hedgehog Review*, 1(1), 1999, p. 40.

Chapter 5   Wellness, Farewell

1 This was the title of a lecture series given by Ivan Illich, as cited in. Metzl, 'Introduction: Why "against health"?', p. 5.

2 Karl Ove Knausgaard, *A Man in Love. My Struggle, Vol. 2* (London: Harvill Secker, 2013), p. 518.

3 Rob Lucas, 'Dreaming in code', *New Left Review*, 62, 2010, p. 128.

4 Susan Sontag, *Illness as Metaphor* (New York: Farrar, Straus and Giroux, 1978), p. 33.

5 Sontag, *Illness as Metaphor*, p. 33.

6 Lucy Phillips, 'British staff far too busy for sick leave', *CIPD*, 25 September 2008.

7 Chris Land and Scott Taylor, 'Surf's up: Work, life, balance and brand in a new age capitalist organization', *Sociology*, 44(3), 2010, pp. 395–413.

8 Cited in Sontag, *Illness as Metaphor*, p. 46.

9 Cited in Sontag, *Illness as Metaphor*, p. 46.

10 Sontag, *Illness as Metaphor*, p. 47.
11 Barbara Ehrenreich, 'Smile! You've got cancer', *Guardian*, 2 January 2010.
12 James Nye, 'The weird world of a Heart Attack Grill girl', *The Daily Mail*, 16 October 2013.
13 Klein, *Eat Fat*, p. 22.
14 Irmgard Tischner, *Fat Lives* (London and New York: Routledge, 2012).
15 Anne Kirkland, 'Think of a hippopotamus: Rights consciousness in the Fat Acceptance movement', *Law and Society Review*, 42(2), 2008, pp. 397–432.
16 Kirkland, 'Think of a hippopotamus', p. 413.
17 Klein, *Eat Fat*, p. 25.
18 Tim Dean, *Unlimited Intimacy: Reflections on the Subculture of Barebacking* (Chicago: University of Chicago Press, 2009), p. 45.
19 Dean, *Unlimited Intimacy*, p. 19.
20 Dean, *Unlimited Intimacy*, p. 66.

Conclusion

1 Bruckner, *Perpetual Euphoria*, p. 231.
2 Zadie Smith, 'Joy', *The New York Review of Books*, 10 January 2013.
3 Martha de Lacey, 'Forget the gym, try a four-hour rave before work: Could teetotal clubbing before breakfast be the kick-start your day needs?', *The Daily Mail*, 1 August 2013.
4 Martha de Lacey, 'Rave yourself fit! The aerobics dance class with a live DJ and plenty of glo-sticks', *The Daily Mail*, 27 August 2013.
5 Peter Fleming, *Resisting Work: The Corporatization of Life and Its Discontents* (Philadelphia: Temple University Press, 2014).
6 Smith, 'Joy'.

Acknowledgements

This book has been in the making for a long time. When we signed the contract several years ago we were planning to write a rather different book than the present one. We want to thank our publisher, Emma Hutchinson, for allowing and even encouraging us to make this turn. We would also like to thank those at Polity Press who have been working on this book, especially Pascal Porcheron and John Thompson. In addition we would like to thank our three anonymous reviewers for taking the time to go through the text in great detail. Thanks to Will Davies for extensive comments, to Steve Brown for helpful suggestions, to Peter Fleming for inspiring discussions about biomorality, to Robyn O'Sullivan for editorial advice, to Justin Dyer for meticulous and sharp editing, and finally to our respective partners, both of whom have helped us shape the ideas of this book.

Index